50 Bread Making Recipes for Home

By: Kelly Johnson

Table of Contents

- Classic French Baguette
- Sourdough Boule
- Whole Wheat Sandwich Bread
- Cinnamon Swirl Bread
- Olive Rosemary Focaccia
- Challah Bread
- Rye Bread
- Brioche Loaf
- Italian Ciabatta
- Irish Soda Bread
- Garlic Knots
- Pumpernickel Bread
- Pretzel Rolls
- Sunflower Seed Bread
- Multigrain Bread
- Cranberry Walnut Bread
- Fennel Seed Breadsticks
- Potato Bread
- Naan Bread
- Cornbread Muffins
- Cheese and Herb Loaf
- Pumpkin Bread
- Jalapeño Cheddar Bread
- Bagels
- Cinnamon Raisin Bread
- Sourdough Discard Crackers
- Pita Bread
- Swedish Cardamom Bread
- Garlic Parmesan Breadsticks
- Everything Bagels
- Whole Wheat Sourdough Sandwich Loaf
- Sesame Seed Bread
- Oatmeal Bread
- Beer Bread
- Irish Brown Bread

- Whole Wheat Dinner Rolls
- Raisin Bran Bread
- Rustic Italian Bread
- Chocolate Babka
- Zucchini Bread
- Anadama Bread
- Blueberry Lemon Bread
- Artisan Olive Bread
- Cheese and Onion Sourdough
- Carrot Cake Bread
- Lemon Poppy Seed Bread
- Spelt Bread
- Apple Cinnamon Bread
- Banana Nut Bread
- Focaccia with Cherry Tomatoes and Basil

Classic French Baguette

Ingredients:

- 500g (about 4 cups) bread flour, plus extra for dusting
- 10g (2 tsp) salt
- 7g (2 ¼ tsp) instant yeast
- 350ml (1 ½ cups) lukewarm water

Instructions:

1. Mixing the Dough:
    - In a large mixing bowl, combine the bread flour and salt.
    - Make a well in the center and add the instant yeast.
    - Pour the lukewarm water into the well.
    - Using a wooden spoon or your hands, gradually incorporate the flour into the water until a shaggy dough forms.
2. Kneading:
    - Transfer the dough to a lightly floured surface.
    - Knead the dough for about 10-15 minutes until it becomes smooth and elastic. You can also use a stand mixer with a dough hook attachment for this step.
    - Shape the dough into a ball.
3. First Rise:
    - Place the dough ball in a lightly greased bowl, cover it with a clean kitchen towel or plastic wrap, and let it rise in a warm, draft-free place for about 1-1.5 hours, or until it doubles in size.
4. Shaping the Baguette:
    - Once the dough has doubled in size, gently deflate it by pressing down on it with your fingertips.
    - Transfer the dough to a lightly floured surface and divide it into three equal portions.
    - Shape each portion into a rough rectangle by pressing it down gently.
    - Fold the top edge of the rectangle down to the center, then fold the bottom edge up to meet it. Press the seam to seal.
    - Roll each piece of dough into a log, about 12-14 inches long.
    - Place the shaped baguettes onto a lightly floured or parchment-lined baking sheet, leaving some space between them.

5. Second Rise:
   - Cover the shaped baguettes loosely with a clean kitchen towel or plastic wrap and let them rise for another 30-45 minutes, or until they have increased in size by about 50%.
6. Preheat the Oven:
   - About 20 minutes before the end of the second rise, preheat your oven to 450°F (230°C). Place an empty baking sheet or a shallow pan on the bottom rack of the oven.
7. Scoring the Baguettes:
   - Using a sharp knife or a bread lame, make 3-4 diagonal slashes along the top of each baguette.
8. Baking:
   - Place the baking sheet with the risen baguettes in the preheated oven.
   - Quickly pour about 1 cup of hot water into the empty baking sheet or pan on the bottom rack of the oven to create steam. Be careful of the steam.
   - Bake the baguettes for 20-25 minutes, or until they are golden brown and sound hollow when tapped on the bottom.
9. Cooling:
   - Transfer the baked baguettes to a wire rack and let them cool completely before slicing.

Enjoy your homemade classic French baguettes! They're perfect for sandwiches, dipping in soups, or simply enjoying with butter.

Sourdough Boule

Ingredients:

- 400g (about 3 cups) bread flour
- 100g (about 3/4 cup) whole wheat flour
- 350g (1 1/2 cups) active sourdough starter (100% hydration)
- 300ml (1 1/4 cups) lukewarm water
- 10g (2 tsp) salt

Instructions:

1. Mixing the Dough:
    - In a large mixing bowl, combine the bread flour, whole wheat flour, and salt.
    - Add the active sourdough starter and lukewarm water to the bowl.
    - Use a wooden spoon or your hands to mix the ingredients until a shaggy dough forms.
2. Autolyse:
    - Let the dough rest in the bowl for 30 minutes to 1 hour. This autolyse period allows the flour to fully hydrate and the gluten to begin developing.
3. Stretch and Fold:
    - After the autolyse, perform a series of stretch and fold actions. To do this, wet your hands and reach under one side of the dough, gently stretching it up and folding it over the top of the dough. Repeat this action from all four sides of the dough.
    - Cover the bowl and let the dough rest for 30 minutes. Repeat the stretch and fold process 3-4 times, at 30-minute intervals.
4. Bulk Fermentation:
    - After the final set of stretch and folds, cover the bowl and let the dough undergo bulk fermentation at room temperature for about 4-6 hours, or until it has increased in volume by about 50-70%. The exact time will depend on the temperature of your kitchen and the activity of your sourdough starter.
5. Shaping the Boule:
    - Once the dough has finished bulk fermentation, transfer it to a lightly floured surface.

- Gently shape the dough into a round boule by folding the edges of the dough towards the center, creating tension on the surface.
- Place the shaped boule into a floured proofing basket or a bowl lined with a floured kitchen towel, seam side up.

6. Final Proof:
   - Cover the shaped boule with a kitchen towel or plastic wrap and let it undergo final proofing at room temperature for 1-2 hours, or until it has increased in size and feels airy to the touch. Alternatively, you can proof the boule in the refrigerator overnight for a slower fermentation and enhanced flavor.

7. Preheat the Oven:
   - About 30 minutes before baking, preheat your oven to 450°F (230°C). Place a Dutch oven or a heavy-bottomed oven-safe pot with a lid inside the oven as it preheats.

8. Baking:
   - Once the oven is preheated, carefully remove the preheated Dutch oven or pot from the oven.
   - Gently transfer the proofed boule into the hot Dutch oven or pot, seam side down.
   - Score the top of the boule with a sharp knife or a bread lame to allow for proper expansion during baking.
   - Cover the Dutch oven or pot with the lid and place it back in the oven.
   - Bake the boule covered for 20-25 minutes.
   - Remove the lid and continue baking the boule uncovered for an additional 20-25 minutes, or until it is golden brown and has a hollow sound when tapped on the bottom.

9. Cooling:
   - Once baked, transfer the sourdough boule to a wire rack and let it cool completely before slicing. Enjoy your freshly baked sourdough boule!

This sourdough boule is perfect for enjoying with soups, salads, or simply with butter and your favorite toppings.

Whole Wheat Sandwich Bread

Ingredients:

- 480g (about 4 cups) whole wheat flour
- 60g (about 1/2 cup) all-purpose flour
- 2 1/4 teaspoons (7g) instant yeast
- 1 1/2 teaspoons (8g) salt
- 1 tablespoon (15g) honey or sugar
- 360ml (1 1/2 cups) lukewarm water
- 3 tablespoons (42g) unsalted butter, softened

Instructions:

1. Mixing the Dough:
    - In a large mixing bowl, combine the whole wheat flour, all-purpose flour, instant yeast, and salt.
    - Add the honey or sugar, lukewarm water, and softened butter to the dry ingredients.
    - Stir the ingredients together until a shaggy dough forms.
2. Kneading:
    - Transfer the dough to a lightly floured surface.
    - Knead the dough for about 8-10 minutes until it becomes smooth and elastic. You can also use a stand mixer with a dough hook attachment for this step.
    - Shape the dough into a ball.
3. First Rise:
    - Place the dough ball in a lightly greased bowl, cover it with a clean kitchen towel or plastic wrap, and let it rise in a warm, draft-free place for about 1-1.5 hours, or until it doubles in size.
4. Shaping the Loaf:
    - Once the dough has doubled in size, gently deflate it by pressing down on it with your fingertips.
    - Transfer the dough to a lightly floured surface and shape it into a loaf. You can do this by flattening the dough into a rectangle and then rolling it up tightly from one end.
    - Pinch the seams and ends to seal.
5. Second Rise:

- Place the shaped loaf into a lightly greased 9x5-inch loaf pan.
- Cover the pan loosely with a clean kitchen towel or plastic wrap and let the dough rise for another 30-45 minutes, or until it has increased in size by about 50%.

6. Preheat the Oven:
    - About 20 minutes before the end of the second rise, preheat your oven to 375°F (190°C).
7. Baking:
    - Once the dough has finished rising, place the loaf pan in the preheated oven.
    - Bake the bread for 30-35 minutes, or until it is golden brown on top and sounds hollow when tapped on the bottom.
    - If the bread is browning too quickly, you can tent it with aluminum foil halfway through baking to prevent over-browning.
8. Cooling:
    - Remove the bread from the oven and let it cool in the pan for 5-10 minutes.
    - Transfer the bread to a wire rack to cool completely before slicing.

Enjoy your freshly baked whole wheat sandwich bread! It's perfect for making sandwiches, toast, or enjoying on its own with a pat of butter.

Cinnamon Swirl Bread

Ingredients:

For the Bread:

- 500g (about 4 cups) all-purpose flour
- 7g (2 1/4 teaspoons) instant yeast
- 50g (1/4 cup) granulated sugar
- 1 teaspoon salt
- 240ml (1 cup) warm milk (about 110°F or 45°C)
- 50g (1/4 cup) unsalted butter, melted
- 1 large egg

For the Cinnamon Filling:

- 100g (1/2 cup) brown sugar
- 2 tablespoons ground cinnamon
- 60g (1/4 cup) unsalted butter, softened

Instructions:

1. Prepare the Dough:
    - In a large mixing bowl, combine the all-purpose flour, instant yeast, granulated sugar, and salt.
    - In a separate bowl, whisk together the warm milk, melted butter, and egg.
    - Pour the wet ingredients into the dry ingredients and mix until a dough forms.
    - Turn the dough out onto a lightly floured surface and knead for about 8-10 minutes, or until the dough is smooth and elastic.
2. First Rise:
    - Place the kneaded dough in a lightly greased bowl, cover it with a clean kitchen towel or plastic wrap, and let it rise in a warm, draft-free place for about 1-1.5 hours, or until it doubles in size.
3. Prepare the Filling:
    - In a small bowl, mix together the brown sugar and ground cinnamon to create the cinnamon filling.

4. Shape the Bread:
   - After the dough has doubled in size, punch it down to release the air.
   - Roll out the dough on a floured surface into a rectangle, about 9x14 inches in size.
   - Spread the softened butter evenly over the surface of the dough.
   - Sprinkle the cinnamon sugar mixture evenly over the buttered dough.
5. Roll and Shape:
   - Starting from one of the shorter ends, tightly roll up the dough into a log.
   - Pinch the seams to seal and tuck the ends under slightly to form a loaf shape.
6. Second Rise:
   - Place the rolled dough seam side down into a lightly greased 9x5-inch loaf pan.
   - Cover the pan loosely with a clean kitchen towel or plastic wrap and let the dough rise for another 45-60 minutes, or until it has risen about 1 inch above the rim of the pan.
7. Preheat the Oven:
   - About 20 minutes before the end of the second rise, preheat your oven to 350°F (175°C).
8. Bake the Bread:
   - Once the dough has finished rising, place the loaf pan in the preheated oven.
   - Bake the bread for 30-35 minutes, or until it is golden brown on top and sounds hollow when tapped on the bottom.
9. Cooling:
   - Remove the bread from the oven and let it cool in the pan for about 10 minutes.
   - Transfer the bread to a wire rack to cool completely before slicing.

Enjoy your delicious homemade Cinnamon Swirl Bread! It's perfect for breakfast or as a sweet treat any time of the day.

Olive Rosemary Focaccia

Ingredients:

For the Dough:

- 500g (about 4 cups) bread flour
- 7g (2 1/4 teaspoons) instant yeast
- 1 tablespoon granulated sugar
- 1 1/2 teaspoons salt
- 350ml (1 1/2 cups) lukewarm water
- 3 tablespoons extra virgin olive oil, plus extra for greasing

For Topping:

- 1/2 cup pitted olives (Kalamata or black olives), sliced
- 2 tablespoons fresh rosemary leaves, chopped
- Coarse sea salt, for sprinkling
- Extra virgin olive oil, for drizzling

Instructions:

1. Prepare the Dough:
    - In a large mixing bowl, combine the bread flour, instant yeast, sugar, and salt.
    - Add the lukewarm water and olive oil to the dry ingredients.
    - Mix until a rough dough forms.
    - Turn the dough out onto a lightly floured surface and knead for about 5-7 minutes until smooth and elastic. Alternatively, you can use a stand mixer with a dough hook attachment for this step.
    - Shape the dough into a ball and place it in a lightly oiled bowl.
    - Cover the bowl with a clean kitchen towel or plastic wrap and let the dough rise in a warm, draft-free place for about 1-1.5 hours, or until it doubles in size.
2. Prepare the Focaccia:
    - Once the dough has doubled in size, punch it down to release the air.

- Transfer the dough to a lightly oiled baking sheet (about 9x13 inches) and gently stretch it to fit the size of the pan.
- Cover the dough loosely with a clean kitchen towel or plastic wrap and let it rise again for about 30-45 minutes.

3. Preheat the Oven:
   - About 20 minutes before baking, preheat your oven to 425°F (220°C).
4. Adding Toppings:
   - After the dough has finished rising, use your fingertips to make dimples all over the surface of the dough.
   - Drizzle the dough generously with extra virgin olive oil, ensuring it fills the dimples.
   - Scatter the sliced olives and chopped rosemary evenly over the dough.
   - Sprinkle coarse sea salt over the top.
5. Baking:
   - Place the baking sheet in the preheated oven and bake the focaccia for 20-25 minutes, or until it is golden brown on top and sounds hollow when tapped on the bottom.
6. Cooling and Serving:
   - Remove the focaccia from the oven and let it cool slightly on the baking sheet.
   - Transfer the focaccia to a wire rack to cool completely before slicing.
   - Serve the olive rosemary focaccia warm or at room temperature. It's delicious on its own or served with a drizzle of balsamic vinegar and extra virgin olive oil.

Enjoy your homemade Olive Rosemary Focaccia! It's perfect as a side dish, appetizer, or for dipping in soups and stews.

Challah Bread

Ingredients:

- 4 cups (500g) bread flour
- 1/4 cup (50g) granulated sugar
- 2 1/4 teaspoons (7g) instant yeast
- 1 teaspoon salt
- 2 large eggs, plus 1 for egg wash
- 1/4 cup (60ml) vegetable oil
- 3/4 cup (180ml) lukewarm water
- Sesame seeds or poppy seeds (optional, for topping)

Instructions:

1. Mixing the Dough:
    - In a large mixing bowl, combine the bread flour, sugar, yeast, and salt.
    - In a separate bowl, whisk together 2 eggs, vegetable oil, and lukewarm water.
    - Pour the wet ingredients into the dry ingredients and mix until a shaggy dough forms.
2. Kneading:
    - Turn the dough out onto a floured surface and knead for about 10 minutes until it becomes smooth and elastic. You can also use a stand mixer with a dough hook attachment for this step.
    - Shape the dough into a ball.
3. First Rise:
    - Place the dough ball in a lightly greased bowl, cover it with a clean kitchen towel or plastic wrap, and let it rise in a warm, draft-free place for about 1-1.5 hours, or until it doubles in size.
4. Dividing and Shaping:
    - After the first rise, punch down the dough to release the air.
    - Divide the dough into three equal portions.
    - Roll each portion into a long rope, about 16-18 inches long.
    - Line up the ropes side by side and pinch them together at one end.
    - Braid the ropes together, pinching the ends together when finished.
5. Second Rise:
    - Place the braided loaf on a baking sheet lined with parchment paper.

- Cover the loaf loosely with a clean kitchen towel or plastic wrap and let it rise for another 30-45 minutes, or until it has increased in size by about 50%.
6. Preheat the Oven:
    - About 20 minutes before baking, preheat your oven to 350°F (175°C).
7. Egg Wash and Topping:
    - Beat the remaining egg in a small bowl with a splash of water to make an egg wash.
    - Brush the egg wash over the top of the risen loaf.
    - If desired, sprinkle sesame seeds or poppy seeds over the top of the loaf for added flavor and decoration.
8. Baking:
    - Place the baking sheet with the risen challah loaf in the preheated oven.
    - Bake for 25-30 minutes, or until the loaf is golden brown on top and sounds hollow when tapped on the bottom.
9. Cooling:
    - Remove the challah from the oven and let it cool on a wire rack before slicing and serving.

Enjoy your homemade challah bread! It's perfect for enjoying fresh or toasted, and makes excellent French toast or bread pudding.

Rye Bread

Ingredients:

- 1 1/2 cups (180g) rye flour
- 2 1/2 cups (300g) bread flour
- 1 packet (7g) active dry yeast
- 1 tablespoon (12g) sugar or honey
- 1 1/2 teaspoons (9g) salt
- 1 1/4 cups (300ml) lukewarm water
- 2 tablespoons (30ml) vegetable oil or melted butter
- 2 tablespoons (30ml) molasses (optional, for flavor)
- Caraway seeds (optional, for flavor)

Instructions:

1. Activate the Yeast:
    - In a small bowl, combine the lukewarm water, sugar (or honey), and active dry yeast. Stir gently and let it sit for about 5-10 minutes until the mixture becomes foamy. This indicates that the yeast is active.
2. Mixing the Dough:
    - In a large mixing bowl, combine the rye flour, bread flour, salt, and optional caraway seeds (if using).
    - Make a well in the center of the dry ingredients and pour in the activated yeast mixture, vegetable oil (or melted butter), and molasses (if using).
    - Stir the ingredients together until a shaggy dough forms.
3. Kneading:
    - Turn the dough out onto a lightly floured surface and knead for about 8-10 minutes until it becomes smooth and elastic. You can also use a stand mixer with a dough hook attachment for this step.
4. First Rise:
    - Place the kneaded dough in a lightly greased bowl, cover it with a clean kitchen towel or plastic wrap, and let it rise in a warm, draft-free place for about 1-1.5 hours, or until it doubles in size.
5. Shaping the Loaf:
    - Once the dough has doubled in size, gently punch it down to release the air.

- Shape the dough into a loaf by rolling it up tightly from one end and pinching the seams to seal.
- Place the shaped loaf into a lightly greased 9x5-inch loaf pan.

6. Second Rise:
    - Cover the loaf pan loosely with a clean kitchen towel or plastic wrap and let the dough rise for another 30-45 minutes, or until it has increased in size by about 50%.
7. Preheat the Oven:
    - About 20 minutes before baking, preheat your oven to 375°F (190°C).
8. Baking:
    - Once the dough has finished rising, place the loaf pan in the preheated oven.
    - Bake the bread for 30-35 minutes, or until it is golden brown on top and sounds hollow when tapped on the bottom.
9. Cooling:
    - Remove the bread from the oven and let it cool in the pan for about 10 minutes.
    - Transfer the bread to a wire rack to cool completely before slicing.

Enjoy your homemade Rye Bread! It's perfect for making sandwiches, toasting, or serving alongside soups and stews.

Brioche Loaf

Ingredients:

- 3 cups (375g) all-purpose flour
- 1/4 cup (50g) granulated sugar
- 1 packet (7g) active dry yeast
- 1 teaspoon salt
- 3 large eggs, at room temperature
- 1/2 cup (115g) unsalted butter, softened
- 1/4 cup (60ml) warm milk
- 1 egg, beaten (for egg wash)

Instructions:

1. Activate the Yeast:
    - In a small bowl, combine the warm milk and a pinch of sugar. Sprinkle the yeast over the milk and let it sit for about 5-10 minutes until the mixture becomes frothy.
2. Mixing the Dough:
    - In a large mixing bowl, combine the all-purpose flour, sugar, and salt.
    - Make a well in the center of the dry ingredients and add the activated yeast mixture.
    - Add the eggs, one at a time, mixing well after each addition.
    - Add the softened butter and knead the dough until it becomes smooth and elastic. You can do this by hand or using a stand mixer with a dough hook attachment.
3. First Rise:
    - Once the dough is well kneaded, shape it into a ball and place it in a lightly greased bowl.
    - Cover the bowl with a clean kitchen towel or plastic wrap and let the dough rise in a warm, draft-free place for about 1-2 hours, or until it doubles in size.
4. Shaping the Loaf:
    - After the dough has doubled in size, gently punch it down to release the air.
    - Transfer the dough to a lightly floured surface and shape it into a loaf.
    - Place the shaped loaf into a lightly greased 9x5-inch loaf pan.

5. Second Rise:
   - Cover the loaf pan loosely with a clean kitchen towel or plastic wrap and let the dough rise for another 30-45 minutes, or until it has increased in size by about 50%.
6. Preheat the Oven:
   - About 20 minutes before baking, preheat your oven to 350°F (175°C).
7. Brush with Egg Wash:
   - Once the dough has finished rising, brush the top of the loaf with beaten egg to give it a shiny finish.
8. Baking:
   - Place the loaf pan in the preheated oven and bake the brioche for 30-35 minutes, or until it is golden brown on top and sounds hollow when tapped on the bottom.
9. Cooling:
   - Remove the brioche from the oven and let it cool in the pan for about 10 minutes.
   - Transfer the brioche to a wire rack to cool completely before slicing.

Enjoy your homemade Brioche Loaf! It's perfect for breakfast, brunch, or as a delicious snack any time of the day.

Italian Ciabatta

Ingredients:

- 500g (about 4 cups) bread flour
- 10g (2 teaspoons) salt
- 7g (2 1/4 teaspoons) instant yeast
- 375ml (1 1/2 cups) lukewarm water
- Extra flour for dusting

Instructions:

1. Mixing the Dough:
    - In a large mixing bowl, combine the bread flour, salt, and instant yeast.
    - Make a well in the center of the dry ingredients and pour in the lukewarm water.
    - Stir the mixture with a wooden spoon until a sticky dough forms.
2. Kneading:
    - Transfer the sticky dough onto a generously floured surface.
    - Dust your hands with flour and begin to knead the dough. Fold the dough over itself, pressing it down with the heel of your hand, and then pushing it away from you. Rotate the dough 90 degrees and repeat the folding and pushing process. Continue kneading for about 10-15 minutes until the dough becomes smooth and elastic. The dough will still be quite wet and sticky, but avoid adding too much extra flour.
3. First Rise:
    - Once the dough is well kneaded, shape it into a rough ball and place it back into the mixing bowl.
    - Cover the bowl with a clean kitchen towel or plastic wrap and let it rise in a warm, draft-free place for about 1-1.5 hours, or until it has doubled in size.
4. Shaping the Loaves:
    - Once the dough has doubled in size, gently deflate it by pressing down on it with your fingertips.
    - Transfer the dough onto a well-floured surface. Use a bench scraper to divide the dough into two equal portions.
    - Working with one portion at a time, gently stretch the dough into a rough rectangle shape, about 8-10 inches long.
5. Second Rise:

- Place the shaped dough onto a parchment-lined baking sheet.
- Cover the dough loosely with a clean kitchen towel or plastic wrap and let it rise for another 30-45 minutes, or until it has increased in size by about 50%.

6. Preheat the Oven:
   - About 20 minutes before baking, preheat your oven to 450°F (230°C). Place an empty baking dish or cast iron skillet on the bottom rack of the oven.
7. Baking:
   - Once the dough has finished rising, lightly dust the tops with flour.
   - Place the baking sheet with the risen ciabatta loaves into the preheated oven.
   - Quickly pour about 1 cup of water into the hot baking dish or skillet on the bottom rack of the oven to create steam. This helps to develop a crisp crust.
   - Bake the ciabatta for 20-25 minutes, or until it is golden brown and sounds hollow when tapped on the bottom.
8. Cooling:
   - Remove the ciabatta from the oven and let it cool on a wire rack for at least 30 minutes before slicing.

Enjoy your homemade Italian Ciabatta bread! It's perfect for sandwiches, bruschetta, or simply served with olive oil and balsamic vinegar for dipping.

Irish Soda Bread

Ingredients:

- 4 cups (500g) all-purpose flour
- 1 teaspoon baking soda
- 1 teaspoon salt
- 1 3/4 cups (420ml) buttermilk
- Optional additions: 1/2 cup (75g) raisins or currants, or 1 tablespoon caraway seeds

Instructions:

1. Preheat the Oven:
    - Preheat your oven to 425°F (220°C). Lightly grease a baking sheet or line it with parchment paper.
2. Mix Dry Ingredients:
    - In a large mixing bowl, whisk together the all-purpose flour, baking soda, and salt until well combined. If you're adding raisins or caraway seeds, stir them into the dry ingredients at this point.
3. Form a Well:
    - Make a well in the center of the dry ingredients and pour in most of the buttermilk.
4. Mix the Dough:
    - Using a wooden spoon or your hands, gently mix the buttermilk into the dry ingredients until you have a soft, slightly sticky dough. Add more buttermilk if needed, but be careful not to overmix.
5. Shape the Dough:
    - Turn the dough out onto a lightly floured surface. Shape it into a round loaf about 6-8 inches in diameter. Use a sharp knife to score a deep cross into the top of the loaf.
6. Bake the Bread:
    - Place the loaf onto the prepared baking sheet. Bake in the preheated oven for 15 minutes.
7. Reduce the Temperature:
    - After 15 minutes, reduce the oven temperature to 400°F (200°C) and continue to bake for another 25-30 minutes, or until the bread is golden brown and sounds hollow when tapped on the bottom.

8. Cooling:
    - Remove the bread from the oven and transfer it to a wire rack to cool completely before slicing.
9. Serve:
    - Enjoy your Irish Soda Bread sliced and served with butter, jam, or alongside a hearty stew.

This simple and delicious bread is a staple of Irish cuisine and is perfect for any occasion, from breakfast to dinner. Enjoy!

Garlic Knots

Ingredients:

For the Dough:

- 2 1/4 cups (280g) all-purpose flour, plus extra for dusting
- 1 teaspoon sugar
- 1 teaspoon salt
- 2 1/4 teaspoons (7g) instant yeast
- 1 cup (240ml) warm water (about 110°F or 45°C)
- 2 tablespoons (30ml) olive oil

For the Garlic Butter:

- 4 tablespoons (60g) unsalted butter, melted
- 4 cloves garlic, minced
- 2 tablespoons fresh parsley, finely chopped (optional)
- Salt, to taste

Instructions:

1. Prepare the Dough:
    - In a large mixing bowl, combine the all-purpose flour, sugar, salt, and instant yeast.
    - Make a well in the center and pour in the warm water and olive oil.
    - Stir the ingredients together until a dough forms.
2. Kneading:
    - Transfer the dough to a lightly floured surface and knead for about 5-7 minutes until it becomes smooth and elastic. You can also use a stand mixer with a dough hook attachment for this step.
3. First Rise:
    - Place the kneaded dough in a lightly greased bowl, cover it with a clean kitchen towel or plastic wrap, and let it rise in a warm, draft-free place for about 1 hour, or until it doubles in size.
4. Shaping the Knots:
    - Once the dough has doubled in size, punch it down to release the air.

- Transfer the dough to a lightly floured surface and divide it into 12 equal portions.
- Roll each portion into a rope about 8 inches long. Tie each rope into a knot and tuck the ends underneath.

5. Second Rise:
   - Place the shaped knots on a baking sheet lined with parchment paper.
   - Cover the knots loosely with a clean kitchen towel or plastic wrap and let them rise for another 30-45 minutes, or until they have increased in size by about 50%.
6. Preheat the Oven:
   - About 20 minutes before baking, preheat your oven to 400°F (200°C).
7. Baking:
   - Once the knots have finished rising, bake them in the preheated oven for 12-15 minutes, or until they are golden brown on top.
8. Prepare the Garlic Butter:
   - While the knots are baking, melt the unsalted butter in a small saucepan over medium heat.
   - Add the minced garlic to the melted butter and cook for 1-2 minutes until fragrant. Be careful not to burn the garlic.
   - Remove the garlic butter from the heat and stir in the chopped parsley (if using) and salt to taste.
9. Finishing:
   - As soon as the knots are done baking, brush them generously with the garlic butter mixture while they're still warm.
   - Serve the garlic knots warm as a delicious appetizer or side dish.

Enjoy your homemade Garlic Knots! They're perfect for serving alongside pasta, soup, or as a tasty snack on their own.

Pumpernickel Bread

Ingredients:

- 2 cups (240g) rye flour
- 1 3/4 cups (210g) whole wheat flour
- 1 cup (120g) bread flour
- 2 tablespoons (15g) cocoa powder
- 2 tablespoons (30g) molasses
- 2 tablespoons (30g) brown sugar
- 2 teaspoons (10g) salt
- 2 1/4 teaspoons (7g) instant yeast
- 1 3/4 cups (420ml) warm water
- 1/4 cup (60ml) vegetable oil
- 1/4 cup (30g) cornmeal (for dusting)

Instructions:

1. Mixing the Dough:
    - In a large mixing bowl, combine the rye flour, whole wheat flour, bread flour, cocoa powder, brown sugar, salt, and instant yeast.
    - Make a well in the center of the dry ingredients and pour in the warm water, molasses, and vegetable oil.
    - Stir the ingredients together until a shaggy dough forms.
2. Kneading:
    - Turn the dough out onto a lightly floured surface and knead for about 8-10 minutes until it becomes smooth and elastic. You can also use a stand mixer with a dough hook attachment for this step.
3. First Rise:
    - Place the kneaded dough in a lightly greased bowl, cover it with a clean kitchen towel or plastic wrap, and let it rise in a warm, draft-free place for about 1-1.5 hours, or until it doubles in size.
4. Shaping the Loaf:
    - Once the dough has doubled in size, gently punch it down to release the air.
    - Shape the dough into a loaf and place it on a baking sheet dusted with cornmeal.
5. Second Rise:

- Cover the loaf loosely with a clean kitchen towel or plastic wrap and let it rise for another 30-45 minutes, or until it has increased in size by about 50%.

6. Preheat the Oven:
    - About 20 minutes before baking, preheat your oven to 350°F (175°C).
7. Baking:
    - Once the dough has finished rising, bake the pumpernickel bread in the preheated oven for 35-40 minutes, or until it is firm and sounds hollow when tapped on the bottom.
8. Cooling:
    - Remove the bread from the oven and let it cool on a wire rack before slicing.

Enjoy your homemade Pumpernickel Bread! It's perfect for sandwiches, toast, or served alongside soups and stews.

Pretzel Rolls

Ingredients:

For the Dough:

- 1 1/2 cups (360ml) warm water (110°F-115°F or 45°C-46°C)
- 1 tablespoon (12g) granulated sugar
- 2 1/4 teaspoons (7g) active dry yeast
- 4 cups (500g) all-purpose flour, plus extra for dusting
- 1 teaspoon salt
- 1/4 cup (60g) unsalted butter, melted
- Coarse sea salt, for topping (optional)

For the Water Bath:

- 9 cups (2.25 liters) water
- 1/2 cup (120ml) baking soda

Instructions:

1. Activate the Yeast:
    - In a small bowl, combine the warm water and sugar. Sprinkle the yeast over the water and let it sit for about 5-10 minutes until it becomes foamy.
2. Prepare the Dough:
    - In a large mixing bowl or the bowl of a stand mixer fitted with a dough hook, combine the flour and salt.
    - Pour the activated yeast mixture and melted butter into the flour mixture.
    - Mix on low speed until the dough comes together. If mixing by hand, use a wooden spoon until a dough forms.
    - Knead the dough for about 5-7 minutes until it is smooth and elastic. If using a stand mixer, knead on low speed.
3. First Rise:
    - Place the dough in a lightly greased bowl, cover it with a clean kitchen towel or plastic wrap, and let it rise in a warm, draft-free place for about 1 hour, or until it doubles in size.
4. Shape the Rolls:

- Once the dough has risen, punch it down to release the air.
- Turn the dough out onto a lightly floured surface and divide it into 12 equal portions.
- Roll each portion into a ball and place them on a baking sheet lined with parchment paper, leaving some space between each roll.

5. Second Rise:
   - Cover the rolls loosely with a clean kitchen towel or plastic wrap and let them rise for another 30-45 minutes, or until they have increased in size by about 50%.
6. Preheat the Oven:
   - About 20 minutes before baking, preheat your oven to 425°F (220°C).
7. Prepare the Water Bath:
   - In a large pot, bring the water and baking soda to a boil.
8. Boil the Rolls:
   - Working with one roll at a time, carefully drop it into the boiling water bath.
   - Boil each roll for about 30 seconds on each side, then remove them using a slotted spoon and place them back on the baking sheet.
9. Bake the Rolls:
   - Once all the rolls have been boiled, sprinkle them with coarse sea salt (if desired).
   - Bake the rolls in the preheated oven for 12-15 minutes, or until they are golden brown on top.
10. Cooling:
    - Remove the rolls from the oven and let them cool on a wire rack for a few minutes before serving.

Enjoy your homemade Pretzel Rolls! They're perfect for sandwiches, burgers, or enjoyed on their own with your favorite dips.

Sunflower Seed Bread

Ingredients:

- 2 cups (240g) bread flour
- 1 cup (120g) whole wheat flour
- 1/2 cup (60g) rye flour
- 1/2 cup (65g) sunflower seeds (plus extra for topping)
- 2 tablespoons (30g) honey or maple syrup
- 2 tablespoons (30g) unsalted butter, melted
- 1 1/4 cups (300ml) warm water
- 2 teaspoons (7g) instant yeast
- 1 teaspoon salt
- Olive oil (for greasing)

Instructions:

1. Activate the Yeast:
    - In a small bowl, combine the warm water and honey (or maple syrup). Sprinkle the yeast over the water mixture and let it sit for about 5-10 minutes until it becomes frothy.
2. Mixing the Dough:
    - In a large mixing bowl, combine the bread flour, whole wheat flour, rye flour, sunflower seeds, and salt.
    - Make a well in the center of the dry ingredients and pour in the activated yeast mixture and melted butter.
    - Stir the ingredients together until a dough forms.
3. Kneading:
    - Turn the dough out onto a lightly floured surface and knead for about 8-10 minutes until it becomes smooth and elastic. You can also use a stand mixer with a dough hook attachment for this step.
4. First Rise:
    - Place the kneaded dough in a lightly greased bowl, cover it with a clean kitchen towel or plastic wrap, and let it rise in a warm, draft-free place for about 1 hour, or until it doubles in size.
5. Shaping the Loaf:
    - Once the dough has doubled in size, gently punch it down to release the air.

- Shape the dough into a loaf and place it in a lightly greased 9x5-inch loaf pan.
6. Second Rise:
    - Cover the loaf loosely with a clean kitchen towel or plastic wrap and let it rise for another 30-45 minutes, or until it has increased in size by about 50%.
7. Preheat the Oven:
    - About 20 minutes before baking, preheat your oven to 375°F (190°C).
8. Topping:
    - Brush the top of the risen loaf with water and sprinkle additional sunflower seeds over the top, gently pressing them into the dough.
9. Baking:
    - Once the dough has finished rising, bake the sunflower seed bread in the preheated oven for 35-40 minutes, or until it is golden brown on top and sounds hollow when tapped on the bottom.
10. Cooling:
    - Remove the bread from the oven and let it cool in the pan for about 10 minutes.
    - Transfer the bread to a wire rack to cool completely before slicing.

Enjoy your homemade Sunflower Seed Bread! It's perfect for sandwiches, toast, or served alongside soups and salads.

Multigrain Bread

Ingredients:

- 1 cup (240ml) warm water (about 110°F or 45°C)
- 2 tablespoons (30ml) honey or maple syrup
- 2 1/4 teaspoons (7g) active dry yeast
- 1 cup (130g) whole wheat flour
- 1/2 cup (65g) bread flour
- 1/2 cup (65g) rye flour
- 1/4 cup (30g) rolled oats, plus extra for topping
- 1/4 cup (30g) flaxseeds
- 1/4 cup (30g) sunflower seeds
- 1/4 cup (30g) pumpkin seeds
- 2 tablespoons (15g) wheat germ
- 2 tablespoons (15g) cornmeal
- 2 tablespoons (30ml) olive oil
- 1 teaspoon salt

Instructions:

1. Activate the Yeast:
    - In a small bowl, combine the warm water and honey (or maple syrup). Sprinkle the yeast over the water mixture and let it sit for about 5-10 minutes until it becomes frothy.
2. Mixing the Dough:
    - In a large mixing bowl, combine the whole wheat flour, bread flour, rye flour, rolled oats, flaxseeds, sunflower seeds, pumpkin seeds, wheat germ, cornmeal, and salt.
    - Make a well in the center of the dry ingredients and pour in the activated yeast mixture and olive oil.
    - Stir the ingredients together until a dough forms.
3. Kneading:
    - Turn the dough out onto a lightly floured surface and knead for about 8-10 minutes until it becomes smooth and elastic. You can also use a stand mixer with a dough hook attachment for this step.
4. First Rise:

- Place the kneaded dough in a lightly greased bowl, cover it with a clean kitchen towel or plastic wrap, and let it rise in a warm, draft-free place for about 1 hour, or until it doubles in size.
5. Shaping the Loaf:
    - Once the dough has doubled in size, gently punch it down to release the air.
    - Shape the dough into a loaf and place it in a lightly greased 9x5-inch loaf pan.
6. Second Rise:
    - Cover the loaf loosely with a clean kitchen towel or plastic wrap and let it rise for another 30-45 minutes, or until it has increased in size by about 50%.
7. Preheat the Oven:
    - About 20 minutes before baking, preheat your oven to 375°F (190°C).
8. Topping:
    - Brush the top of the risen loaf with water and sprinkle additional rolled oats over the top, gently pressing them into the dough.
9. Baking:
    - Once the dough has finished rising, bake the multigrain bread in the preheated oven for 35-40 minutes, or until it is golden brown on top and sounds hollow when tapped on the bottom.
10. Cooling:
    - Remove the bread from the oven and let it cool in the pan for about 10 minutes.
    - Transfer the bread to a wire rack to cool completely before slicing.

Enjoy your homemade Multigrain Bread! It's packed with nutritious seeds and grains and is perfect for sandwiches, toast, or served alongside soups and salads.

Cranberry Walnut Bread

Ingredients:

- 2 cups (250g) all-purpose flour
- 1/2 cup (100g) granulated sugar
- 1 1/2 teaspoons baking powder
- 1/2 teaspoon baking soda
- 1/2 teaspoon salt
- 1 cup (120g) chopped walnuts
- 1 cup (100g) dried cranberries
- 1 large egg
- 3/4 cup (180ml) buttermilk
- 1/4 cup (60ml) vegetable oil
- 1 teaspoon vanilla extract
- Zest of 1 orange (optional)

Instructions:

1. Preheat the Oven:
    - Preheat your oven to 350°F (175°C). Grease and flour a 9x5-inch loaf pan, or line it with parchment paper.
2. Mix Dry Ingredients:
    - In a large mixing bowl, whisk together the flour, sugar, baking powder, baking soda, and salt until well combined.
3. Add Walnuts and Cranberries:
    - Stir in the chopped walnuts and dried cranberries until evenly distributed throughout the dry ingredients.
4. Mix Wet Ingredients:
    - In a separate bowl, beat the egg lightly. Add the buttermilk, vegetable oil, vanilla extract, and orange zest (if using). Mix until well combined.
5. Combine Wet and Dry Ingredients:
    - Pour the wet ingredients into the dry ingredients. Stir until just combined. Be careful not to overmix; it's okay if the batter is slightly lumpy.
6. Transfer to Loaf Pan:
    - Pour the batter into the prepared loaf pan, spreading it evenly.
7. Bake:

- Bake in the preheated oven for 50-60 minutes, or until a toothpick inserted into the center comes out clean and the top is golden brown.

8. Cooling:
    - Allow the bread to cool in the pan for about 10 minutes before transferring it to a wire rack to cool completely.
9. Slice and Serve:
    - Once cooled, slice the Cranberry Walnut Bread and serve it as desired. It's delicious toasted with a bit of butter, or simply enjoyed on its own.
10. Storage:
    - Store any leftover bread in an airtight container at room temperature for up to 3 days, or freeze for longer storage.

Enjoy your homemade Cranberry Walnut Bread! It's perfect for breakfast, brunch, or as a delightful snack any time of day.

Fennel Seed Breadsticks

Ingredients:

- 2 cups (250g) all-purpose flour
- 1 teaspoon salt
- 1 tablespoon sugar
- 1 tablespoon fennel seeds
- 1 teaspoon active dry yeast
- 3/4 cup (180ml) warm water
- 2 tablespoons olive oil
- Extra olive oil for brushing
- Coarse sea salt, for sprinkling (optional)

Instructions:

1. Activate the Yeast:
    - In a small bowl, combine the warm water and sugar. Sprinkle the yeast over the water and let it sit for about 5-10 minutes until it becomes frothy.
2. Mixing the Dough:
    - In a large mixing bowl, combine the all-purpose flour, salt, fennel seeds, and activated yeast mixture.
    - Stir the ingredients together until a dough forms.
3. Kneading:
    - Turn the dough out onto a lightly floured surface and knead for about 5 minutes until it becomes smooth and elastic.
4. First Rise:
    - Place the kneaded dough in a lightly greased bowl, cover it with a clean kitchen towel or plastic wrap, and let it rise in a warm, draft-free place for about 1 hour, or until it doubles in size.
5. Shaping the Breadsticks:
    - Once the dough has doubled in size, punch it down to release the air.
    - Divide the dough into 12 equal portions.
    - Roll each portion into a thin rope, about 8-10 inches long. Place the ropes onto a baking sheet lined with parchment paper, leaving some space between each breadstick.
6. Second Rise:

- Cover the breadsticks loosely with a clean kitchen towel or plastic wrap and let them rise for another 30-45 minutes, or until they have increased in size by about 50%.
7. Preheat the Oven:
    - About 20 minutes before baking, preheat your oven to 375°F (190°C).
8. Baking:
    - Once the breadsticks have finished rising, brush them lightly with olive oil and sprinkle with coarse sea salt if desired.
    - Bake the breadsticks in the preheated oven for 12-15 minutes, or until they are golden brown and crispy.
9. Cooling:
    - Remove the breadsticks from the oven and let them cool on a wire rack for a few minutes before serving.

Enjoy your homemade Fennel Seed Breadsticks! They're perfect for dipping in marinara sauce, hummus, or served alongside salads and soups.

Potato Bread

Ingredients:

- 1 cup mashed potatoes (about 2 medium potatoes)
- 1 cup warm water (about 110°F or 45°C)
- 2 tablespoons sugar
- 2 1/4 teaspoons active dry yeast
- 1/4 cup (60ml) vegetable oil or melted butter
- 1 teaspoon salt
- 4 cups (500g) bread flour, plus extra for dusting

Instructions:

1. Prepare the Mashed Potatoes:
    - Peel and chop the potatoes into small cubes. Boil them in water until tender, then drain and mash them until smooth. Measure out 1 cup of mashed potatoes for the recipe.
2. Activate the Yeast:
    - In a small bowl, combine the warm water and sugar. Sprinkle the yeast over the water mixture and let it sit for about 5-10 minutes until it becomes frothy.
3. Mixing the Dough:
    - In a large mixing bowl or the bowl of a stand mixer fitted with a dough hook attachment, combine the mashed potatoes, activated yeast mixture, vegetable oil (or melted butter), and salt.
    - Gradually add the bread flour, mixing until a dough forms.
4. Kneading:
    - Turn the dough out onto a lightly floured surface and knead for about 8-10 minutes until it becomes smooth and elastic. You can also knead the dough in a stand mixer with a dough hook attachment on low speed.
5. First Rise:
    - Place the kneaded dough in a lightly greased bowl, cover it with a clean kitchen towel or plastic wrap, and let it rise in a warm, draft-free place for about 1-1.5 hours, or until it doubles in size.
6. Shaping the Loaf:
    - Once the dough has doubled in size, gently punch it down to release the air.

- Shape the dough into a loaf and place it in a lightly greased 9x5-inch loaf pan.
7. Second Rise:
    - Cover the loaf loosely with a clean kitchen towel or plastic wrap and let it rise for another 30-45 minutes, or until it has increased in size by about 50%.
8. Preheat the Oven:
    - About 20 minutes before baking, preheat your oven to 375°F (190°C).
9. Baking:
    - Once the dough has finished rising, bake the potato bread in the preheated oven for 30-35 minutes, or until it is golden brown on top and sounds hollow when tapped on the bottom.
10. Cooling:
    - Remove the bread from the oven and let it cool in the pan for about 10 minutes.
    - Transfer the bread to a wire rack to cool completely before slicing.

Enjoy your homemade Potato Bread! It's perfect for sandwiches, toast, or served alongside soups and stews.

Naan Bread

Ingredients:

- 2 cups (250g) all-purpose flour, plus extra for dusting
- 1 teaspoon active dry yeast
- 1 teaspoon sugar
- 1/2 teaspoon salt
- 1/4 teaspoon baking powder
- 2 tablespoons plain yogurt
- 2 tablespoons olive oil or melted butter
- 1/2 cup (120ml) warm milk
- 2-3 tablespoons water (if needed)

Optional Toppings:

- Garlic butter (melted butter mixed with minced garlic)
- Chopped cilantro (coriander) leaves
- Nigella seeds (kalonji)
- Sesame seeds

Instructions:

1. Activate the Yeast:
    - In a small bowl, combine the warm milk, sugar, and yeast. Let it sit for about 5-10 minutes until the mixture becomes frothy.
2. Mix Dry Ingredients:
    - In a large mixing bowl, combine the all-purpose flour, salt, and baking powder.
3. Combine Wet Ingredients:
    - Make a well in the center of the dry ingredients and pour in the activated yeast mixture, yogurt, and olive oil (or melted butter).
    - Stir the ingredients together until a dough forms. If the dough is too dry, add water, 1 tablespoon at a time, until you get a soft, slightly sticky dough.
4. Kneading:
    - Turn the dough out onto a lightly floured surface and knead for about 5-7 minutes until it becomes smooth and elastic.
5. First Rise:

- Place the kneaded dough in a lightly greased bowl, cover it with a clean kitchen towel or plastic wrap, and let it rise in a warm, draft-free place for about 1-2 hours, or until it doubles in size.

6. Divide and Shape:
   - Once the dough has doubled in size, punch it down to release the air.
   - Divide the dough into 6-8 equal portions and shape each portion into a smooth ball.
7. Second Rise:
   - Place the dough balls on a lightly floured surface, cover them with a clean kitchen towel, and let them rest for another 15-20 minutes.
8. Rolling Out:
   - Roll out each dough ball into an oval or round shape, about 1/4 inch (6mm) thick. You can use a rolling pin for this step.
9. Cooking:
   - Heat a non-stick skillet or griddle over medium-high heat. Once hot, place a rolled-out naan onto the skillet and cook for about 1-2 minutes, or until bubbles form on the surface and the bottom is golden brown.
10. Flip and Finish:
    - Flip the naan and cook for another 1-2 minutes until the other side is golden brown and cooked through.
    - Optionally, brush the cooked naan with garlic butter and sprinkle with chopped cilantro, nigella seeds, or sesame seeds before serving.
11. Repeat:
    - Repeat the process with the remaining dough balls, stacking the cooked naan and covering them with a clean kitchen towel to keep them warm.
12. Serve:
    - Serve the warm naan bread alongside your favorite Indian dishes, or use them to make wraps or sandwiches.

Enjoy your homemade Naan Bread! It's perfect for soaking up curries or enjoying as a tasty snack.

Cornbread Muffins

Ingredients:

- 1 cup (120g) cornmeal
- 1 cup (125g) all-purpose flour
- 1/4 cup (50g) granulated sugar
- 1 tablespoon baking powder
- 1/2 teaspoon salt
- 1 cup (240ml) milk
- 1/4 cup (60ml) vegetable oil or melted butter
- 1 large egg

Instructions:

1. Preheat the Oven:
    - Preheat your oven to 400°F (200°C). Grease or line a muffin tin with paper liners.
2. Mix Dry Ingredients:
    - In a large mixing bowl, combine the cornmeal, all-purpose flour, sugar, baking powder, and salt. Mix well.
3. Combine Wet Ingredients:
    - In a separate bowl, whisk together the milk, vegetable oil (or melted butter), and egg until well combined.
4. Combine Wet and Dry Ingredients:
    - Pour the wet ingredients into the bowl of dry ingredients. Stir until just combined. Do not overmix; a few lumps are okay.
5. Fill Muffin Cups:
    - Divide the batter evenly among the prepared muffin cups, filling each about 2/3 full.
6. Bake:
    - Place the muffin tin in the preheated oven and bake for 15-20 minutes, or until the tops are golden brown and a toothpick inserted into the center comes out clean.
7. Cooling:
    - Remove the muffins from the oven and let them cool in the pan for a few minutes. Then transfer them to a wire rack to cool completely.
8. Serve:

- Serve the cornbread muffins warm or at room temperature. They are delicious on their own, or you can serve them with butter, honey, or your favorite jam.

These cornbread muffins are perfect for breakfast, brunch, or as a side dish for soups, stews, and chili. Enjoy!

Cheese and Herb Loaf

Ingredients:

- 3 cups (360g) all-purpose flour
- 1 tablespoon granulated sugar
- 1 tablespoon baking powder
- 1 teaspoon salt
- 1/2 cup (115g) unsalted butter, cold and cubed
- 1 1/2 cups (170g) grated cheese (such as cheddar, Gouda, or a blend)
- 2 tablespoons chopped fresh herbs (such as parsley, chives, or thyme)
- 1 cup (240ml) milk
- 1 large egg, beaten (for egg wash)
- Additional grated cheese and chopped herbs for topping (optional)

Instructions:

1. Preheat the Oven:
    - Preheat your oven to 375°F (190°C). Grease or line a loaf pan with parchment paper.
2. Mix Dry Ingredients:
    - In a large mixing bowl, combine the all-purpose flour, sugar, baking powder, and salt. Mix well.
3. Incorporate Butter:
    - Add the cold cubed butter to the flour mixture. Using a pastry cutter or your fingers, cut the butter into the flour until the mixture resembles coarse crumbs.
4. Add Cheese and Herbs:
    - Stir in the grated cheese and chopped herbs until evenly distributed throughout the flour mixture.
5. Combine Wet Ingredients:
    - Make a well in the center of the dry ingredients and pour in the milk. Stir until just combined. The dough will be sticky.
6. Form the Loaf:
    - Transfer the dough to the prepared loaf pan and press it down gently to fill the pan evenly.
7. Brush with Egg Wash:

- Brush the top of the loaf with the beaten egg. This will give it a shiny, golden crust.
8. Optional Toppings:
    - Sprinkle additional grated cheese and chopped herbs over the top of the loaf, if desired, for extra flavor and visual appeal.
9. Bake:
    - Place the loaf pan in the preheated oven and bake for 40-45 minutes, or until the loaf is golden brown and a toothpick inserted into the center comes out clean.
10. Cooling:
    - Remove the loaf from the oven and let it cool in the pan for about 10 minutes. Then transfer it to a wire rack to cool completely before slicing.
11. Serve:
    - Slice the Cheese and Herb Loaf and serve it warm or at room temperature. It's delicious on its own or served alongside soups, salads, or as part of a cheese platter.

Enjoy your homemade Cheese and Herb Loaf! It's perfect for any occasion and sure to be a hit with cheese and herb lovers alike.

Pumpkin Bread

Ingredients:

- 1 3/4 cups (220g) all-purpose flour
- 1 teaspoon baking soda
- 1/2 teaspoon baking powder
- 1 teaspoon ground cinnamon
- 1/2 teaspoon ground nutmeg
- 1/2 teaspoon ground cloves
- 1/2 teaspoon salt
- 1/2 cup (120ml) vegetable oil or melted butter
- 1 1/2 cups (300g) granulated sugar
- 2 large eggs
- 1 cup (240g) canned pumpkin puree
- 1/3 cup (80ml) water
- 1/2 cup (120g) chopped nuts (optional)
- 1/2 cup (80g) raisins or chocolate chips (optional)

Instructions:

1. Preheat the Oven:
    - Preheat your oven to 350°F (175°C). Grease and flour a 9x5-inch loaf pan, or line it with parchment paper.
2. Mix Dry Ingredients:
    - In a medium mixing bowl, whisk together the flour, baking soda, baking powder, cinnamon, nutmeg, cloves, and salt until well combined.
3. Mix Wet Ingredients:
    - In a large mixing bowl, beat together the oil (or melted butter) and sugar until well combined.
    - Add the eggs one at a time, beating well after each addition.
    - Stir in the pumpkin puree and water until smooth.
4. Combine Wet and Dry Ingredients:
    - Gradually add the dry ingredients to the wet ingredients, stirring until just combined. Do not overmix.
    - If using, fold in the chopped nuts, raisins, or chocolate chips until evenly distributed in the batter.
5. Transfer to Loaf Pan:

- Pour the batter into the prepared loaf pan, spreading it evenly.
6. Bake:
    - Place the loaf pan in the preheated oven and bake for 60-70 minutes, or until a toothpick inserted into the center comes out clean.
7. Cooling:
    - Remove the pumpkin bread from the oven and let it cool in the pan for about 10 minutes.
    - Then transfer the bread to a wire rack to cool completely before slicing.
8. Serve:
    - Slice the Pumpkin Bread and serve it warm or at room temperature. It's delicious on its own, or you can spread butter or cream cheese on top for extra flavor.

Enjoy your homemade Pumpkin Bread! It's perfect for breakfast, snacking, or as a tasty treat any time of day.

Jalapeño Cheddar Bread

Ingredients:

- 3 cups (360g) all-purpose flour
- 1 tablespoon sugar
- 1 tablespoon baking powder
- 1 teaspoon salt
- 1 cup (120g) shredded cheddar cheese
- 1-2 jalapeño peppers, seeded and finely chopped
- 1 cup (240ml) milk
- 1/4 cup (60ml) vegetable oil or melted butter
- 1 large egg, beaten

Instructions:

1. Preheat the Oven:
    - Preheat your oven to 350°F (175°C). Grease and flour a 9x5-inch loaf pan, or line it with parchment paper.
2. Mix Dry Ingredients:
    - In a large mixing bowl, combine the all-purpose flour, sugar, baking powder, and salt. Stir in the shredded cheddar cheese and chopped jalapeño peppers until evenly distributed.
3. Combine Wet Ingredients:
    - In a separate bowl, whisk together the milk, vegetable oil (or melted butter), and beaten egg until well combined.
4. Combine Wet and Dry Ingredients:
    - Pour the wet ingredients into the bowl of dry ingredients. Stir until just combined. Do not overmix; a few lumps are okay.
5. Transfer to Loaf Pan:
    - Pour the batter into the prepared loaf pan, spreading it evenly.
6. Bake:
    - Place the loaf pan in the preheated oven and bake for 45-55 minutes, or until the top is golden brown and a toothpick inserted into the center comes out clean.
7. Cooling:
    - Remove the bread from the oven and let it cool in the pan for about 10 minutes. Then transfer it to a wire rack to cool completely before slicing.

8. Serve:
    - Slice the Jalapeño Cheddar Bread and serve it warm or at room temperature. It's delicious on its own or served with soups, stews, or chili.

Enjoy your homemade Jalapeño Cheddar Bread! It's packed with cheesy and spicy flavors, perfect for adding a kick to your meal.

Bagels

Ingredients:

- 4 cups (500g) bread flour
- 2 teaspoons instant yeast
- 2 tablespoons granulated sugar
- 1 1/2 teaspoons salt
- 1 1/4 cups (300ml) warm water
- 2 tablespoons vegetable oil
- 1 egg, beaten (for egg wash)
- Optional toppings: sesame seeds, poppy seeds, dried onion flakes, coarse salt, etc.

Instructions:

1. Mix Dough:
    - In a large mixing bowl, combine the bread flour, instant yeast, sugar, and salt. Mix well.
    - Make a well in the center of the dry ingredients and pour in the warm water and vegetable oil.
    - Stir until a dough forms.
2. Knead Dough:
    - Turn the dough out onto a lightly floured surface and knead for about 10 minutes until it becomes smooth and elastic. Alternatively, you can knead the dough in a stand mixer with a dough hook attachment for 6-8 minutes.
3. First Rise:
    - Place the kneaded dough in a lightly greased bowl, cover it with a clean kitchen towel or plastic wrap, and let it rise in a warm, draft-free place for about 1 hour, or until it doubles in size.
4. Divide and Shape:
    - Once the dough has doubled in size, punch it down to release the air.
    - Divide the dough into 8 equal portions.
    - Roll each portion into a smooth ball. Use your thumb to poke a hole through the center of each ball, then gently stretch the hole to form a bagel shape.
5. Second Rise:

- Place the shaped bagels on a lightly greased baking sheet, leaving some space between each one.
- Cover the bagels loosely with a clean kitchen towel or plastic wrap and let them rise for another 20-30 minutes.

6. Preheat Oven:
    - While the bagels are rising, preheat your oven to 400°F (200°C). Bring a large pot of water to a boil.
7. Boil Bagels:
    - Once the bagels have finished rising, carefully place them, a few at a time, into the boiling water.
    - Boil the bagels for about 1-2 minutes on each side. The longer you boil them, the chewier they'll be.
8. Egg Wash and Toppings:
    - Remove the boiled bagels from the water using a slotted spoon and place them back on the baking sheet.
    - Brush each bagel with beaten egg and sprinkle with your desired toppings, if using.
9. Bake:
    - Bake the bagels in the preheated oven for 20-25 minutes, or until they are golden brown and sound hollow when tapped on the bottom.
10. Cooling:
    - Remove the bagels from the oven and let them cool on a wire rack for a few minutes before serving.

Enjoy your homemade bagels! They're delicious toasted and served with cream cheese, smoked salmon, or your favorite sandwich fillings.

Cinnamon Raisin Bread

Ingredients:

- 1 cup (240ml) warm milk
- 2 1/4 teaspoons (7g) active dry yeast
- 1/4 cup (50g) granulated sugar
- 1/4 cup (60g) unsalted butter, melted
- 1 teaspoon salt
- 1 large egg
- 4 cups (500g) all-purpose flour
- 1 cup (150g) raisins
- 1/4 cup (50g) packed brown sugar
- 2 teaspoons ground cinnamon
- 2 tablespoons unsalted butter, melted (for brushing)

Instructions:

1. Activate the Yeast:
    - In a small bowl, combine the warm milk, active dry yeast, and a pinch of sugar. Let it sit for about 5-10 minutes until the mixture becomes frothy.
2. Mix Dough:
    - In a large mixing bowl, combine the frothy yeast mixture, granulated sugar, melted butter, salt, and egg. Mix well.
    - Gradually add the flour, stirring until a dough forms.
3. Knead Dough:
    - Turn the dough out onto a lightly floured surface and knead for about 8-10 minutes until it becomes smooth and elastic. Alternatively, you can knead the dough in a stand mixer with a dough hook attachment.
4. First Rise:
    - Place the kneaded dough in a lightly greased bowl, cover it with a clean kitchen towel or plastic wrap, and let it rise in a warm, draft-free place for about 1-1.5 hours, or until it doubles in size.
5. Prepare Filling:
    - In a small bowl, combine the brown sugar and ground cinnamon.
6. Shape Loaf:
    - Punch down the risen dough to release the air.
    - Roll the dough out into a large rectangle, about 1/2 inch (1.25 cm) thick.

- Brush the melted butter over the surface of the dough, then sprinkle the cinnamon-sugar mixture evenly over the buttered dough.
- Scatter the raisins evenly over the cinnamon-sugar mixture.

7. Roll Up Dough:
    - Starting from one long edge, tightly roll up the dough into a log shape.
8. Second Rise:
    - Place the rolled-up dough seam side down in a lightly greased loaf pan.
    - Cover the loaf pan loosely with a clean kitchen towel or plastic wrap and let it rise for another 30-45 minutes, or until it has increased in size by about 50%.
9. Preheat Oven:
    - About 20 minutes before baking, preheat your oven to 350°F (175°C).
10. Bake:
    - Once the dough has finished rising, bake the cinnamon raisin bread in the preheated oven for 35-40 minutes, or until it is golden brown on top and sounds hollow when tapped on the bottom.
11. Cooling:
    - Remove the bread from the oven and let it cool in the pan for about 10 minutes.
    - Transfer the bread to a wire rack to cool completely before slicing.

Enjoy your homemade Cinnamon Raisin Bread! It's perfect for toasting and spreading with butter or cream cheese for a delicious breakfast or snack.

Sourdough Discard Crackers

Ingredients:

- 1 cup (240g) sourdough discard
- 2 tablespoons olive oil
- 1 teaspoon salt (adjust to taste)
- Optional: herbs, spices, grated cheese, or seeds for flavor (such as rosemary, thyme, garlic powder, onion powder, sesame seeds, etc.)

Instructions:

1. Preheat Oven:
    - Preheat your oven to 350°F (175°C). Line a baking sheet with parchment paper or a silicone baking mat.
2. Mix Ingredients:
    - In a mixing bowl, combine the sourdough discard, olive oil, salt, and any optional flavorings you desire. Mix until well combined.
3. Roll Out Dough:
    - Transfer the dough onto a lightly floured surface. Roll out the dough into a thin, even layer. Aim for a thickness of about 1/8 inch (3mm) or less.
4. Cut into Shapes:
    - Use a knife or pizza cutter to cut the dough into desired shapes. You can make squares, rectangles, or use cookie cutters for fun shapes.
5. Prick with Fork:
    - Use a fork to prick each cracker a few times. This will prevent them from puffing up too much during baking.
6. Transfer to Baking Sheet:
    - Carefully transfer the cut crackers onto the prepared baking sheet, leaving a little space between each cracker.
7. Bake:
    - Place the baking sheet in the preheated oven and bake for 15-20 minutes, or until the crackers are golden brown and crispy.
8. Cooling:
    - Remove the crackers from the oven and let them cool on the baking sheet for a few minutes.
9. Serve:

- Once cooled, transfer the crackers to a wire rack to cool completely. They will crisp up further as they cool.
- Serve the sourdough discard crackers as a snack on their own, or pair them with cheese, dips, or spreads.

These crackers can be stored in an airtight container at room temperature for up to a week. Enjoy your homemade sourdough discard crackers!

Pita Bread

Ingredients:

- 2 1/4 teaspoons (7g) active dry yeast
- 1 teaspoon granulated sugar
- 1 1/4 cups (300ml) warm water (about 110°F or 45°C)
- 3 cups (360g) all-purpose flour, plus extra for dusting
- 1 teaspoon salt
- 2 tablespoons olive oil

Instructions:

1. Activate the Yeast:
    - In a small bowl, combine the warm water, sugar, and active dry yeast. Stir gently and let it sit for about 5-10 minutes until it becomes frothy.
2. Mix Dough:
    - In a large mixing bowl, combine the flour and salt. Make a well in the center and pour in the activated yeast mixture and olive oil.
    - Stir the ingredients together until a shaggy dough forms.
3. Knead Dough:
    - Turn the dough out onto a lightly floured surface. Knead the dough for about 5-7 minutes until it becomes smooth and elastic. Add a little more flour if the dough is too sticky.
4. First Rise:
    - Place the kneaded dough in a lightly greased bowl, cover it with a clean kitchen towel or plastic wrap, and let it rise in a warm, draft-free place for about 1-1.5 hours, or until it doubles in size.
5. Preheat Oven:
    - Preheat your oven to 475°F (245°C). If you have a pizza stone, place it in the oven to preheat as well.
6. Divide Dough:
    - Punch down the risen dough to release the air. Divide the dough into 8 equal portions.
7. Shape Pitas:
    - On a lightly floured surface, roll out each portion of dough into a circle about 1/4 inch (6mm) thick. Try to make them as even as possible.
8. Second Rise:

- Place the rolled-out pitas on a lightly floured surface or parchment paper. Cover them loosely with a clean kitchen towel or plastic wrap and let them rise for another 20-30 minutes.

9. Bake:
    - Once the pitas have finished rising, carefully transfer them to the preheated oven or pizza stone.
    - Bake for 5-7 minutes, or until they puff up and become golden brown on top.
10. Cooling:
    - Remove the pitas from the oven and let them cool on a wire rack for a few minutes.
11. Serve:
    - Serve the homemade pita bread warm or at room temperature. They're delicious filled with your favorite sandwich fillings, dipped in hummus, or used for wraps and pizzas.

Enjoy your homemade pita bread! They're perfect for any meal and are sure to impress with their fresh, fluffy texture.

Swedish Cardamom Bread

For the Filling:

- 1/4 cup (50g) granulated sugar
- 2 teaspoons ground cardamom
- 1/4 cup (60g) unsalted butter, softened

For the Glaze:

- 1/4 cup (60ml) water
- 1/4 cup (50g) granulated sugar
- 1 teaspoon ground cardamom

Instructions:

1. Prepare the Dough:
    - In a small saucepan, heat the milk and butter over low heat until the butter has melted. Remove from heat and let it cool until it reaches lukewarm temperature.
    - In a large mixing bowl, combine the lukewarm milk mixture, sugar, salt, and yeast. Let it sit for 5-10 minutes until the yeast becomes foamy.
    - Add the flour and ground cardamom to the yeast mixture, and knead until a smooth dough forms. You can do this by hand or using a stand mixer with a dough hook attachment.
    - Place the dough in a lightly greased bowl, cover it with a clean kitchen towel or plastic wrap, and let it rise in a warm, draft-free place for about 1-1.5 hours, or until it doubles in size.
2. Prepare the Filling:
    - In a small bowl, mix together the sugar and ground cardamom for the filling.
    - Once the dough has risen, punch it down to release the air. On a lightly floured surface, roll out the dough into a large rectangle, about 1/4 inch (6mm) thick.
    - Spread the softened butter evenly over the rolled-out dough, then sprinkle the sugar-cardamom mixture on top.
3. Shape the Bread:

- Starting from one long edge, tightly roll up the dough into a log shape. Slice the log into 12 equal pieces.
4. Second Rise:
    - Place the sliced pieces on a baking sheet lined with parchment paper, leaving some space between each piece.
    - Cover the dough loosely with a clean kitchen towel or plastic wrap and let it rise for another 30-45 minutes.
5. Preheat the Oven:
    - About 20 minutes before baking, preheat your oven to 375°F (190°C).
6. Bake:
    - Once the dough has finished rising, bake the Swedish Cardamom Bread in the preheated oven for 15-20 minutes, or until golden brown.
7. Prepare the Glaze:
    - While the bread is baking, prepare the glaze. In a small saucepan, combine the water, sugar, and ground cardamom. Heat over medium heat until the sugar has dissolved, then remove from heat.
8. Glaze the Bread:
    - As soon as the bread comes out of the oven, brush the warm glaze over the top of each piece.
9. Cooling and Serving:
    - Let the Swedish Cardamom Bread cool slightly on a wire rack before serving. Enjoy warm with a cup of coffee or tea.

These Swedish Cardamom Breads are fragrant, soft, and deliciously sweet, making them a perfect treat for any occasion!

Garlic Parmesan Breadsticks

Ingredients:

For the Dough:

- 2 1/4 teaspoons (1 packet) active dry yeast
- 1 teaspoon granulated sugar
- 1 cup (240ml) warm water (about 110°F/45°C)
- 2 1/2 cups (300g) all-purpose flour
- 1 teaspoon salt
- 2 tablespoons olive oil

For the Topping:

- 4 tablespoons unsalted butter, melted
- 2 cloves garlic, minced
- 1/4 cup (25g) grated Parmesan cheese
- 1 teaspoon dried oregano
- 1/2 teaspoon garlic powder
- Salt, to taste
- Fresh parsley, finely chopped (optional, for garnish)

Instructions:

1. Activate the Yeast:
     - In a small bowl, combine the warm water, sugar, and yeast. Stir gently and let it sit for about 5-10 minutes until it becomes frothy.
2. Prepare the Dough:
     - In a large mixing bowl, combine the flour and salt. Make a well in the center and pour in the activated yeast mixture and olive oil.
     - Stir the ingredients together until a dough forms. Turn the dough out onto a lightly floured surface and knead for about 5-7 minutes until it becomes smooth and elastic. If the dough is too sticky, add a little more flour as needed.
3. First Rise:

- Place the kneaded dough in a lightly greased bowl, cover it with a clean kitchen towel or plastic wrap, and let it rise in a warm, draft-free place for about 1 hour, or until it doubles in size.
4. Preheat Oven:
    - Preheat your oven to 425°F (220°C). Line a baking sheet with parchment paper.
5. Shape the Breadsticks:
    - Punch down the risen dough to release the air. Divide the dough into 12 equal portions.
    - Roll each portion into a rope about 8-10 inches (20-25cm) long and place them on the prepared baking sheet, leaving some space between each breadstick.
6. Second Rise:
    - Cover the shaped breadsticks loosely with a clean kitchen towel or plastic wrap and let them rise for another 20-30 minutes.
7. Bake:
    - Once the breadsticks have finished rising, bake them in the preheated oven for 12-15 minutes, or until they are golden brown and cooked through.
8. Prepare the Topping:
    - In a small bowl, mix together the melted butter, minced garlic, grated Parmesan cheese, dried oregano, garlic powder, and salt.
9. Coat the Breadsticks:
    - As soon as the breadsticks come out of the oven, brush them generously with the garlic Parmesan butter mixture while they're still warm.
10. Garnish and Serve:
    - If desired, sprinkle the freshly chopped parsley over the breadsticks for garnish.
    - Serve the Garlic Parmesan Breadsticks warm as a delicious appetizer or side dish. They're perfect for dipping in marinara sauce, garlic butter, or your favorite dip.

Enjoy your homemade Garlic Parmesan Breadsticks! They're crispy, flavorful, and incredibly satisfying.

Everything Bagels

Ingredients:

For the Dough:

- 1 1/2 cups (360ml) warm water (about 110°F/45°C)
- 2 1/4 teaspoons (1 packet) active dry yeast
- 1 tablespoon granulated sugar
- 4 cups (500g) bread flour (plus extra for kneading)
- 1 1/2 teaspoons salt

For the Boiling Solution:

- 2 quarts (1.9 liters) water
- 2 tablespoons granulated sugar
- 1 tablespoon baking soda

For the Everything Bagel Topping:

- 2 tablespoons sesame seeds
- 2 tablespoons poppy seeds
- 1 tablespoon dried minced garlic
- 1 tablespoon dried minced onion
- 1 teaspoon coarse salt

Instructions:

1. Activate the Yeast:
   - In a small bowl, combine the warm water, sugar, and yeast. Stir gently and let it sit for about 5-10 minutes until it becomes frothy.
2. Prepare the Dough:
   - In a large mixing bowl, combine the bread flour and salt. Make a well in the center and pour in the activated yeast mixture.
   - Stir the ingredients together until a dough forms. Turn the dough out onto a lightly floured surface and knead for about 8-10 minutes until it becomes

smooth and elastic. If the dough is too sticky, add a little more flour as needed.

3. **First Rise:**
   - Place the kneaded dough in a lightly greased bowl, cover it with a clean kitchen towel or plastic wrap, and let it rise in a warm, draft-free place for about 1 hour, or until it doubles in size.

4. **Shape the Bagels:**
   - Once the dough has risen, punch it down to release the air. Divide the dough into 12 equal portions.
   - Roll each portion into a smooth ball, then use your finger to poke a hole through the center. Stretch and shape the dough to form a bagel shape. Make the hole slightly larger than you want the finished bagel to be, as it will shrink during boiling and baking.

5. **Second Rise:**
   - Place the shaped bagels on a baking sheet lined with parchment paper, leaving some space between each bagel.
   - Cover the bagels loosely with a clean kitchen towel or plastic wrap and let them rise for another 20-30 minutes.

6. **Preheat Oven and Prepare Boiling Solution:**
   - About 20 minutes before baking, preheat your oven to 425°F (220°C).
   - In a large pot, bring the water, sugar, and baking soda to a boil.

7. **Boil the Bagels:**
   - Once the water is boiling, carefully place the risen bagels into the boiling water, a few at a time. Boil for about 1-2 minutes on each side, flipping them halfway through. This boiling step helps to create the chewy texture and shiny crust of traditional bagels.

8. **Apply Toppings:**
   - While the bagels are still wet from boiling, sprinkle them generously with the Everything Bagel Topping mixture. You can also dip the top of each bagel into the topping mixture if you prefer.

9. **Bake:**
   - Transfer the topped bagels back to the baking sheet lined with parchment paper. Bake in the preheated oven for 20-25 minutes, or until the bagels are golden brown and sound hollow when tapped on the bottom.

10. **Cooling and Serving:**
    - Let the Everything Bagels cool on a wire rack for a few minutes before serving. Enjoy them warm or toasted with cream cheese, smoked salmon, or your favorite bagel toppings.

These homemade Everything Bagels are deliciously chewy on the inside with a crispy crust and packed with flavor from the Everything Bagel Topping. Enjoy!

Whole Wheat Sourdough Sandwich Loaf

Ingredients:

For the Sourdough Starter:

- 1 cup (120g) whole wheat flour
- 1/2 cup (120ml) lukewarm water
- 2 tablespoons active sourdough starter (fed and active)

For the Dough:

- 2 cups (240g) whole wheat flour
- 1 1/2 cups (180g) bread flour (or all-purpose flour)
- 1 1/4 cups (300ml) lukewarm water
- 2 tablespoons honey (or maple syrup)
- 2 tablespoons olive oil (or melted butter)
- 2 teaspoons salt

Instructions:

1. Prepare the Sourdough Starter:
    - In a large mixing bowl, combine the whole wheat flour, lukewarm water, and active sourdough starter. Stir until well combined.
    - Cover the bowl loosely with a clean kitchen towel or plastic wrap and let it sit at room temperature for 8-12 hours, or until bubbly and active.
2. Mix the Dough:
    - Once the sourdough starter is bubbly and active, add the remaining ingredients for the dough: whole wheat flour, bread flour, lukewarm water, honey, olive oil, and salt.
    - Stir the ingredients together until a shaggy dough forms.
3. Knead the Dough:
    - Turn the dough out onto a lightly floured surface. Knead the dough for about 10-15 minutes until it becomes smooth and elastic. You can also knead the dough in a stand mixer with a dough hook attachment for 8-10 minutes.
4. First Rise:

- Place the kneaded dough in a lightly greased bowl. Cover it with a clean kitchen towel or plastic wrap and let it rise in a warm, draft-free place for about 2-3 hours, or until it doubles in size.

5. Shape the Loaf:
    - Once the dough has doubled in size, punch it down to release the air. Turn the dough out onto a lightly floured surface and shape it into a loaf.
    - Place the shaped dough into a lightly greased 9x5-inch (23x13cm) loaf pan. Cover the pan loosely with a clean kitchen towel or plastic wrap and let it rise for another 1-2 hours, or until it rises just above the rim of the pan.
6. Preheat the Oven:
    - About 20 minutes before baking, preheat your oven to 375°F (190°C).
7. Bake the Loaf:
    - Once the loaf has finished rising, place it in the preheated oven and bake for 40-45 minutes, or until the loaf is golden brown on top and sounds hollow when tapped on the bottom.
8. Cooling and Serving:
    - Remove the loaf from the oven and let it cool in the pan for about 10 minutes. Then transfer it to a wire rack to cool completely before slicing.
    - Once cooled, slice the Whole Wheat Sourdough Sandwich Loaf and enjoy it as is or toasted with your favorite sandwich fillings.

This homemade Whole Wheat Sourdough Sandwich Loaf is perfect for sandwiches, toast, or enjoying on its own. Its rich flavor and wholesome texture make it a delicious and nutritious choice for any meal.

Sesame Seed Bread

Ingredients:

- 2 cups (240g) bread flour
- 1 cup (120g) whole wheat flour
- 1 packet (2 1/4 teaspoons) active dry yeast
- 1 tablespoon sugar
- 1 teaspoon salt
- 1 cup (240ml) warm water (about 110°F/45°C)
- 2 tablespoons olive oil
- 1/4 cup (30g) sesame seeds (plus extra for topping)
- 1 egg, beaten (for egg wash, optional)

Instructions:

1. Activate the Yeast:
    - In a small bowl, combine the warm water, sugar, and yeast. Stir gently and let it sit for about 5-10 minutes until it becomes frothy.
2. Mix Dough:
    - In a large mixing bowl, combine the bread flour, whole wheat flour, salt, and sesame seeds.
    - Make a well in the center of the dry ingredients and pour in the activated yeast mixture and olive oil.
    - Stir the ingredients together until a dough forms.
3. Knead Dough:
    - Turn the dough out onto a lightly floured surface and knead for about 8-10 minutes until it becomes smooth and elastic. Alternatively, you can knead the dough in a stand mixer with a dough hook attachment.
4. First Rise:
    - Place the kneaded dough in a lightly greased bowl, cover it with a clean kitchen towel or plastic wrap, and let it rise in a warm, draft-free place for about 1-1.5 hours, or until it doubles in size.
5. Shape the Loaf:
    - Once the dough has doubled in size, punch it down to release the air. Shape the dough into a loaf and place it in a lightly greased 9x5-inch (23x13cm) loaf pan.
6. Second Rise:

- Cover the loaf pan loosely with a clean kitchen towel or plastic wrap and let it rise for another 30-45 minutes, or until it rises just above the rim of the pan.
7. Preheat Oven:
    - About 20 minutes before baking, preheat your oven to 375°F (190°C).
8. Egg Wash and Sesame Seed Topping:
    - If desired, brush the top of the risen loaf with beaten egg and sprinkle with additional sesame seeds for a shiny and flavorful crust.
9. Bake:
    - Place the loaf pan in the preheated oven and bake for 30-35 minutes, or until the bread is golden brown on top and sounds hollow when tapped on the bottom.
10. Cooling and Serving:
    - Remove the bread from the oven and let it cool in the pan for about 10 minutes. Then transfer it to a wire rack to cool completely before slicing.
    - Slice the Sesame Seed Bread and enjoy it plain, toasted, or with your favorite spreads and toppings.

This homemade Sesame Seed Bread is flavorful, nutty, and perfect for sandwiches, toast, or enjoying on its own. Enjoy!

Oatmeal Bread

Ingredients:

- 1 cup (240ml) warm water (about 110°F/45°C)
- 2 tablespoons honey or maple syrup
- 2 1/4 teaspoons (1 packet) active dry yeast
- 1 cup (90g) old-fashioned rolled oats
- 1/4 cup (60ml) milk (dairy or plant-based)
- 2 tablespoons unsalted butter or coconut oil, melted
- 1 1/2 teaspoons salt
- 3 cups (360g) bread flour (or all-purpose flour), plus extra for kneading

Instructions:

1. Activate the Yeast:
    - In a large mixing bowl, combine the warm water, honey or maple syrup, and active dry yeast. Stir gently and let it sit for about 5-10 minutes until it becomes frothy.
2. Prepare the Oatmeal:
    - In a separate bowl, pour the milk over the rolled oats and let them soak for about 10 minutes.
3. Mix Dough:
    - Once the yeast mixture is frothy, add the soaked oats with milk, melted butter or coconut oil, and salt to the bowl.
    - Gradually add the flour, stirring until a shaggy dough forms.
4. Knead Dough:
    - Turn the dough out onto a lightly floured surface. Knead the dough for about 8-10 minutes until it becomes smooth and elastic. Add a little more flour if the dough is too sticky.
5. First Rise:
    - Place the kneaded dough in a lightly greased bowl, cover it with a clean kitchen towel or plastic wrap, and let it rise in a warm, draft-free place for about 1-1.5 hours, or until it doubles in size.
6. Shape the Loaf:
    - Once the dough has doubled in size, punch it down to release the air. Shape the dough into a loaf and place it in a lightly greased 9x5-inch (23x13cm) loaf pan.

7. Second Rise:
   - Cover the loaf pan loosely with a clean kitchen towel or plastic wrap and let it rise for another 30-45 minutes, or until it rises just above the rim of the pan.
8. Preheat Oven:
   - About 20 minutes before baking, preheat your oven to 350°F (175°C).
9. Bake:
   - Place the loaf pan in the preheated oven and bake for 30-35 minutes, or until the bread is golden brown on top and sounds hollow when tapped on the bottom.
10. Cooling and Serving:
    - Remove the bread from the oven and let it cool in the pan for about 10 minutes. Then transfer it to a wire rack to cool completely before slicing.
    - Slice the Oatmeal Bread and enjoy it plain, toasted, or with your favorite spreads and toppings.

This homemade Oatmeal Bread is hearty, wholesome, and perfect for sandwiches, toast, or enjoying on its own. Enjoy!

Beer Bread

Ingredients:

- 3 cups (360g) all-purpose flour
- 1/4 cup (50g) granulated sugar
- 1 tablespoon baking powder
- 1 teaspoon salt
- 12 ounces (1 1/2 cups or 355ml) beer, preferably room temperature
- 1/4 cup (60g) unsalted butter, melted

Instructions:

1. Preheat Oven:
    - Preheat your oven to 375°F (190°C). Grease a 9x5-inch (23x13cm) loaf pan or line it with parchment paper.
2. Mix Dry Ingredients:
    - In a large mixing bowl, whisk together the all-purpose flour, sugar, baking powder, and salt until well combined.
3. Add Beer:
    - Pour the beer into the dry ingredients. Stir gently until just combined. Be careful not to overmix; a few lumps are okay.
4. Transfer to Pan:
    - Pour the batter into the prepared loaf pan and spread it out evenly.
5. Add Melted Butter:
    - Drizzle the melted butter evenly over the top of the batter in the loaf pan.
6. Bake:
    - Place the loaf pan in the preheated oven and bake for 45-55 minutes, or until the top is golden brown and a toothpick inserted into the center comes out clean.
7. Cooling and Serving:
    - Remove the beer bread from the oven and let it cool in the pan for about 10 minutes.
    - Transfer the bread to a wire rack to cool completely before slicing.
    - Slice and serve the beer bread as desired. It's delicious on its own, with butter, or alongside soups and stews.

This Beer Bread is incredibly easy to make and has a wonderfully crisp crust with a soft and fluffy interior. Enjoy!

Irish Brown Bread

Ingredients:

- 2 cups (240g) whole wheat flour
- 1 cup (120g) all-purpose flour
- 1 teaspoon baking soda
- 1 teaspoon salt
- 1 3/4 cups (420ml) buttermilk
- 2 tablespoons honey or molasses (optional)
- Extra flour for dusting

Instructions:

1. Preheat Oven:
    - Preheat your oven to 425°F (220°C). Lightly grease a baking sheet or line it with parchment paper.
2. Mix Dry Ingredients:
    - In a large mixing bowl, whisk together the whole wheat flour, all-purpose flour, baking soda, and salt until well combined.
3. Add Wet Ingredients:
    - Make a well in the center of the dry ingredients and pour in the buttermilk (and honey or molasses, if using).
    - Using a wooden spoon or your hands, mix the ingredients until a rough dough forms. The dough should be slightly sticky but manageable. Add a little more buttermilk or flour if needed to achieve the right consistency.
4. Shape the Dough:
    - Turn the dough out onto a lightly floured surface. Knead it gently for a minute or two until it comes together into a smooth ball.
5. Form the Loaf:
    - Shape the dough into a round loaf, about 6-8 inches (15-20cm) in diameter. Place it on the prepared baking sheet.
6. Score the Top:
    - Use a sharp knife to score a deep cross into the top of the loaf. This helps the bread to bake evenly and allows steam to escape.
7. Bake:
    - Bake the bread in the preheated oven for 15 minutes, then reduce the oven temperature to 400°F (200°C) and continue baking for another 25-30

minutes, or until the bread is golden brown and sounds hollow when tapped on the bottom.
8. Cooling:
    - Remove the bread from the oven and transfer it to a wire rack to cool completely before slicing.
9. Serve:
    - Slice the Irish Brown Bread and serve it with butter, cheese, jam, or your favorite toppings. It's perfect for breakfast, brunch, or as a snack.

Enjoy your homemade Irish Brown Bread! It's hearty, wholesome, and full of flavor.

Whole Wheat Dinner Rolls

Ingredients:

- 1 cup (240ml) warm water (about 110°F/45°C)
- 2 1/4 teaspoons (1 packet) active dry yeast
- 2 tablespoons honey or maple syrup
- 2 tablespoons olive oil or melted butter
- 1 teaspoon salt
- 2 1/2 cups (300g) whole wheat flour
- 1/2 cup (60g) all-purpose flour (plus extra for kneading)

Instructions:

1. Activate the Yeast:
    - In a large mixing bowl, combine the warm water, honey or maple syrup, and active dry yeast. Stir gently and let it sit for about 5-10 minutes until it becomes frothy.
2. Mix Dough:
    - Add the olive oil or melted butter and salt to the yeast mixture. Stir to combine.
    - Gradually add the whole wheat flour and all-purpose flour, stirring until a dough forms.
3. Knead Dough:
    - Turn the dough out onto a lightly floured surface. Knead the dough for about 8-10 minutes until it becomes smooth and elastic. Add a little more flour if the dough is too sticky.
4. First Rise:
    - Place the kneaded dough in a lightly greased bowl. Cover it with a clean kitchen towel or plastic wrap and let it rise in a warm, draft-free place for about 1 hour, or until it doubles in size.
5. Shape the Rolls:
    - Once the dough has doubled in size, punch it down to release the air. Turn the dough out onto a lightly floured surface.
    - Divide the dough into 12 equal portions and shape each portion into a smooth ball.
6. Second Rise:

- Place the shaped rolls on a baking sheet lined with parchment paper, leaving some space between each roll.
- Cover the rolls loosely with a clean kitchen towel or plastic wrap and let them rise for another 30-45 minutes, or until they rise just above the rim of the pan.

7. Preheat Oven:
    - About 20 minutes before baking, preheat your oven to 375°F (190°C).
8. Bake:
    - Once the rolls have finished rising, place them in the preheated oven and bake for 15-20 minutes, or until they are golden brown on top.
9. Cooling and Serving:
    - Remove the rolls from the oven and let them cool on a wire rack for a few minutes before serving.
    - Serve the Whole Wheat Dinner Rolls warm with butter or your favorite toppings.

These Whole Wheat Dinner Rolls are soft, fluffy, and perfect for serving alongside soups, stews, or as a side dish for any meal. Enjoy!

Raisin Bran Bread

Ingredients:

- 1 1/2 cups (360ml) buttermilk
- 1/4 cup (60ml) vegetable oil
- 1/4 cup (85g) honey or maple syrup
- 1 large egg
- 1 1/2 cups (180g) all-purpose flour
- 1 cup (120g) whole wheat flour
- 1/2 teaspoon salt
- 1 tablespoon baking powder
- 1 teaspoon baking soda
- 1 cup (120g) raisins
- 1 1/2 cups (45g) bran flakes cereal

Instructions:

1. Preheat Oven:
    - Preheat your oven to 350°F (175°C). Grease a 9x5-inch (23x13cm) loaf pan or line it with parchment paper.
2. Mix Wet Ingredients:
    - In a large mixing bowl, whisk together the buttermilk, vegetable oil, honey or maple syrup, and egg until well combined.
3. Combine Dry Ingredients:
    - In a separate bowl, sift together the all-purpose flour, whole wheat flour, salt, baking powder, and baking soda.
4. Mix Batter:
    - Gradually add the dry ingredients to the wet ingredients, stirring until just combined.
    - Fold in the raisins and bran flakes cereal until evenly distributed throughout the batter.
5. Transfer to Pan:
    - Pour the batter into the prepared loaf pan and spread it out evenly.
6. Bake:
    - Bake the bread in the preheated oven for 45-50 minutes, or until a toothpick inserted into the center comes out clean.
7. Cooling and Serving:

- Remove the bread from the oven and let it cool in the pan for about 10 minutes.
- Transfer the bread to a wire rack to cool completely before slicing.
- Slice the Raisin Bran Bread and serve it toasted with butter or your favorite spreads.

This Raisin Bran Bread is hearty, slightly sweet, and packed with wholesome ingredients. Enjoy it for breakfast, as a snack, or as part of your favorite sandwich!

Rustic Italian Bread

Ingredients:

- 1 1/2 cups (360ml) warm water (about 110°F/45°C)
- 2 1/4 teaspoons (1 packet) active dry yeast
- 1 tablespoon sugar
- 4 cups (480g) bread flour
- 2 teaspoons salt
- 2 tablespoons olive oil
- Cornmeal or semolina flour (for dusting)

Instructions:

1. Activate the Yeast:
    - In a large mixing bowl, combine the warm water, sugar, and active dry yeast. Stir gently and let it sit for about 5-10 minutes until it becomes frothy.
2. Mix Dough:
    - Add the bread flour, salt, and olive oil to the yeast mixture. Stir until a shaggy dough forms.
3. Knead Dough:
    - Turn the dough out onto a lightly floured surface. Knead the dough for about 8-10 minutes until it becomes smooth and elastic.
4. First Rise:
    - Place the kneaded dough in a lightly greased bowl. Cover it with a clean kitchen towel or plastic wrap and let it rise in a warm, draft-free place for about 1-1.5 hours, or until it doubles in size.
5. Shape the Loaf:
    - Once the dough has doubled in size, punch it down to release the air. Shape the dough into a round or oval loaf.
6. Second Rise:
    - Place the shaped loaf on a baking sheet dusted with cornmeal or semolina flour. Cover it loosely with a clean kitchen towel or plastic wrap and let it rise for another 30-45 minutes.
7. Preheat Oven:

- About 20 minutes before baking, preheat your oven to 425°F (220°C). Place an empty baking dish or cast iron skillet on the bottom rack of the oven.

8. Score the Bread:
   - Use a sharp knife or razor blade to score the top of the loaf with a few diagonal slashes.
9. Bake:
   - Once the loaf has finished rising, place it in the preheated oven. Pour about 1 cup of hot water into the empty baking dish or cast iron skillet to create steam in the oven.
   - Bake the bread for 25-30 minutes, or until it is golden brown and sounds hollow when tapped on the bottom.
10. Cooling and Serving:
    - Remove the bread from the oven and let it cool on a wire rack for at least 30 minutes before slicing.
    - Slice the Rustic Italian Bread and serve it warm with olive oil, balsamic vinegar, or your favorite toppings.

This Rustic Italian Bread has a crispy crust and a soft, chewy interior, perfect for enjoying with soups, salads, pasta, or as a standalone snack. Enjoy!

Chocolate Babka

Ingredients:

For the Dough:

- 4 cups (480g) all-purpose flour, plus extra for dusting
- 1/2 cup (100g) granulated sugar
- 2 1/4 teaspoons (1 packet) active dry yeast
- 3/4 cup (180ml) warm milk (about 110°F/45°C)
- 2 large eggs, room temperature
- 1/2 cup (115g) unsalted butter, melted and cooled
- 1 teaspoon vanilla extract
- 1/2 teaspoon salt

For the Chocolate Filling:

- 1 cup (175g) semisweet chocolate chips or chopped chocolate
- 1/2 cup (115g) unsalted butter, softened
- 1/2 cup (100g) granulated sugar
- 1/4 cup (25g) unsweetened cocoa powder
- 1 teaspoon ground cinnamon (optional)

For the Syrup:

- 1/4 cup (60ml) water
- 1/4 cup (50g) granulated sugar

Instructions:

1. Activate the Yeast:
    - In a small bowl, combine the warm milk, 1 tablespoon of sugar, and active dry yeast. Stir gently and let it sit for about 5-10 minutes until it becomes frothy.
2. Make the Dough:
    - In a large mixing bowl or the bowl of a stand mixer fitted with a dough hook attachment, combine the flour, remaining sugar, and salt.
    - Add the activated yeast mixture, melted butter, eggs, and vanilla extract to the dry ingredients. Mix until a dough forms.
3. Knead the Dough:

- Knead the dough for about 8-10 minutes until it becomes smooth and elastic. If the dough is too sticky, add a little more flour, 1 tablespoon at a time.

4. First Rise:
   - Place the kneaded dough in a greased bowl, cover it with a clean kitchen towel or plastic wrap, and let it rise in a warm, draft-free place for about 1-1.5 hours, or until it doubles in size.

5. Make the Filling:
   - While the dough is rising, prepare the chocolate filling. In a medium bowl, mix together the softened butter, sugar, cocoa powder, and ground cinnamon (if using) until smooth.

6. Assemble the Babka:
   - Once the dough has doubled in size, punch it down to release the air. Roll the dough out on a lightly floured surface into a large rectangle, about 16x20 inches (40x50cm).
   - Spread the chocolate filling evenly over the dough, leaving a small border around the edges.

7. Roll and Twist:
   - Starting from one long side, tightly roll the dough into a log. Use a sharp knife to cut the log in half lengthwise, exposing the layers of dough and filling.
   - Twist the two halves together, keeping the exposed layers facing upwards.

8. Second Rise:
   - Transfer the twisted dough to a greased loaf pan or a parchment-lined baking sheet. Cover it loosely with a clean kitchen towel or plastic wrap and let it rise for another 30-45 minutes.

9. Preheat Oven:
   - About 20 minutes before baking, preheat your oven to 350°F (175°C).

10. Bake:
    - Once the babka has finished rising, bake it in the preheated oven for 30-35 minutes, or until it is golden brown and cooked through.

11. Make the Syrup:
    - While the babka is baking, prepare the syrup. In a small saucepan, combine the water and sugar. Bring to a simmer over medium heat, stirring until the sugar dissolves. Remove from heat and set aside.

12. Brush with Syrup:
    - As soon as the babka comes out of the oven, brush it generously with the prepared syrup while it's still warm. This adds shine and sweetness to the crust.

13. Cooling and Serving:
    - Let the babka cool in the pan for about 10 minutes, then transfer it to a wire rack to cool completely before slicing.
    - Slice the Chocolate Babka and serve it as a delicious sweet treat or dessert.

This Chocolate Babka is best enjoyed fresh but can also be stored in an airtight container at room temperature for up to 3 days. Enjoy the rich chocolate flavor and beautiful swirls in every bite!

Zucchini Bread

Ingredients:

- 2 cups (250g) all-purpose flour
- 1 teaspoon baking soda
- 1 teaspoon baking powder
- 1/2 teaspoon salt
- 1 teaspoon ground cinnamon
- 1/2 teaspoon ground nutmeg (optional)
- 2 large eggs
- 1/2 cup (100g) granulated sugar
- 1/2 cup (100g) brown sugar, packed
- 1/2 cup (120ml) vegetable oil or melted coconut oil
- 1 teaspoon vanilla extract
- 1 1/2 cups (180g) grated zucchini (about 1 medium zucchini)
- 1/2 cup (50g) chopped nuts (walnuts or pecans), optional
- 1/2 cup (75g) raisins or chocolate chips, optional

Instructions:

1. Preheat Oven and Prepare Pan:
    - Preheat your oven to 350°F (175°C). Grease a 9x5-inch (23x13cm) loaf pan or line it with parchment paper.
2. Mix Dry Ingredients:
    - In a large mixing bowl, whisk together the all-purpose flour, baking soda, baking powder, salt, ground cinnamon, and ground nutmeg (if using). Set aside.
3. Prepare Wet Ingredients:
    - In another bowl, beat the eggs lightly. Add the granulated sugar, brown sugar, vegetable oil, and vanilla extract. Mix until well combined.
4. Combine Wet and Dry Ingredients:
    - Pour the wet ingredients into the dry ingredients. Stir until just combined. Be careful not to overmix; a few lumps are okay.
5. Add Zucchini and Optional Ingredients:
    - Fold in the grated zucchini until evenly distributed throughout the batter.
    - If using, fold in the chopped nuts and raisins or chocolate chips.
6. Transfer to Pan:
    - Pour the batter into the prepared loaf pan and spread it out evenly.

7. Bake:
    - Bake in the preheated oven for 50-60 minutes, or until a toothpick inserted into the center comes out clean.
8. Cooling and Serving:
    - Remove the zucchini bread from the oven and let it cool in the pan for about 10 minutes. Then transfer it to a wire rack to cool completely before slicing.
    - Slice the zucchini bread and serve it plain, toasted, or with a smear of butter. Enjoy!

This Zucchini Bread is moist, flavorful, and perfect for breakfast, snack, or dessert. It's a great way to use up surplus zucchinis and is sure to be a hit with family and friends!

Anadama Bread

Ingredients:

- 1 cup (240ml) warm water (about 110°F/45°C)
- 1/2 cup (120ml) milk, warmed
- 1/4 cup (85g) molasses
- 3 tablespoons unsalted butter, softened
- 1 1/2 teaspoons salt
- 1/2 cup (60g) cornmeal
- 3 1/2 cups (420g) bread flour
- 2 1/4 teaspoons (1 packet) active dry yeast

Instructions:

1. Activate the Yeast:
    - In a small bowl, combine the warm water and yeast. Let it sit for about 5-10 minutes until it becomes frothy.
2. Mix Wet Ingredients:
    - In a large mixing bowl or the bowl of a stand mixer fitted with a dough hook attachment, combine the warm milk, molasses, softened butter, and salt. Mix until well combined.
3. Add Dry Ingredients:
    - Gradually add the cornmeal and bread flour to the wet ingredients, mixing until a dough forms.
4. Knead Dough:
    - Turn the dough out onto a lightly floured surface. Knead the dough for about 8-10 minutes until it becomes smooth and elastic. Alternatively, you can knead the dough in a stand mixer for 6-8 minutes.
5. First Rise:
    - Place the kneaded dough in a lightly greased bowl. Cover it with a clean kitchen towel or plastic wrap and let it rise in a warm, draft-free place for about 1-1.5 hours, or until it doubles in size.
6. Shape the Loaf:
    - Once the dough has doubled in size, punch it down to release the air. Shape the dough into a loaf and place it in a greased 9x5-inch (23x13cm) loaf pan.
7. Second Rise:

- Cover the loaf pan loosely with a clean kitchen towel or plastic wrap and let it rise for another 30-45 minutes, or until it rises just above the rim of the pan.

8. Preheat Oven:
    - About 20 minutes before baking, preheat your oven to 375°F (190°C).
9. Bake:
    - Once the loaf has finished rising, place it in the preheated oven and bake for 35-40 minutes, or until it is golden brown on top and sounds hollow when tapped on the bottom.
10. Cooling and Serving:
    - Remove the bread from the oven and let it cool in the pan for about 10 minutes. Then transfer it to a wire rack to cool completely before slicing.
    - Slice the Anadama Bread and serve it plain, toasted, or with your favorite spreads.

This Anadama Bread is sweet, hearty, and perfect for enjoying as a snack or alongside soups and stews. Enjoy!

Blueberry Lemon Bread

Ingredients:

- 1 1/2 cups (180g) all-purpose flour
- 1 teaspoon baking powder
- 1/4 teaspoon baking soda
- 1/4 teaspoon salt
- 1/2 cup (115g) unsalted butter, softened
- 3/4 cup (150g) granulated sugar
- 2 large eggs, room temperature
- 1/2 cup (120ml) plain yogurt or sour cream
- Zest of 1 lemon
- 1 tablespoon fresh lemon juice
- 1 teaspoon vanilla extract
- 1 cup (150g) fresh or frozen blueberries, tossed in 1 tablespoon of flour (to prevent sinking)

For the Lemon Glaze:

- 1/2 cup (60g) powdered sugar
- 1-2 tablespoons fresh lemon juice

Instructions:

1. Preheat Oven and Prepare Pan:
    - Preheat your oven to 350°F (175°C). Grease a 9x5-inch (23x13cm) loaf pan or line it with parchment paper.
2. Mix Dry Ingredients:
    - In a medium bowl, whisk together the all-purpose flour, baking powder, baking soda, and salt. Set aside.
3. Cream Butter and Sugar:
    - In a large mixing bowl, cream together the softened butter and granulated sugar until light and fluffy.
4. Add Wet Ingredients:
    - Beat in the eggs, one at a time, until well combined. Add the plain yogurt or sour cream, lemon zest, lemon juice, and vanilla extract. Mix until smooth.
5. Combine Wet and Dry Ingredients:

- Gradually add the dry ingredients to the wet ingredients, mixing until just combined. Do not overmix.
6. Fold in Blueberries:
    - Gently fold the flour-coated blueberries into the batter until evenly distributed.
7. Transfer to Pan:
    - Pour the batter into the prepared loaf pan and spread it out evenly.
8. Bake:
    - Bake in the preheated oven for 50-60 minutes, or until a toothpick inserted into the center comes out clean. If the top starts to brown too quickly, you can loosely cover it with aluminum foil.
9. Cooling:
    - Remove the bread from the oven and let it cool in the pan for about 10 minutes. Then transfer it to a wire rack to cool completely.
10. Prepare Glaze:
    - In a small bowl, whisk together the powdered sugar and lemon juice until smooth. Adjust the consistency by adding more lemon juice if too thick or more powdered sugar if too thin.
11. Drizzle Glaze:
    - Once the bread has cooled, drizzle the lemon glaze over the top.
12. Slice and Serve:
    - Slice the Blueberry Lemon Bread and serve it as a delicious breakfast, snack, or dessert.

This Blueberry Lemon Bread is bursting with juicy blueberries and bright lemon flavor.

It's perfect for any occasion and is sure to be a hit with family and friends! Enjoy!

Artisan Olive Bread

Ingredients:

- 3 cups (360g) bread flour
- 1 1/2 teaspoons instant yeast
- 1 teaspoon salt
- 1 tablespoon granulated sugar
- 1 cup (240ml) lukewarm water
- 1/4 cup (60ml) extra virgin olive oil
- 1 cup (150g) pitted olives (such as Kalamata or green olives), chopped
- Optional: additional whole olives for topping

Instructions:

1. Activate the Yeast:
    - In a small bowl, mix together the lukewarm water and sugar until the sugar is dissolved. Sprinkle the instant yeast over the water and let it sit for about 5-10 minutes until foamy.
2. Mix the Dough:
    - In a large mixing bowl, combine the bread flour and salt. Make a well in the center and pour in the yeast mixture and olive oil. Stir until a dough forms.
3. Knead the Dough:
    - Turn the dough out onto a lightly floured surface. Knead the dough for about 8-10 minutes until it becomes smooth and elastic. Alternatively, you can knead the dough in a stand mixer fitted with a dough hook attachment.
4. First Rise:
    - Place the kneaded dough in a lightly greased bowl. Cover it with a clean kitchen towel or plastic wrap and let it rise in a warm, draft-free place for about 1-1.5 hours, or until it doubles in size.
5. Add Olives:
    - Once the dough has doubled in size, gently punch it down to release the air. Fold in the chopped olives until evenly distributed throughout the dough.
6. Shape the Loaf:

- Shape the dough into a round or oval loaf and place it on a parchment-lined baking sheet. If desired, press additional whole olives into the surface of the dough.

7. Second Rise:
    - Cover the shaped loaf loosely with a clean kitchen towel or plastic wrap and let it rise for another 30-45 minutes, or until it rises just above the rim of the pan.
8. Preheat Oven:
    - About 20 minutes before baking, preheat your oven to 400°F (200°C).
9. Bake:
    - Once the loaf has finished rising, bake it in the preheated oven for 25-30 minutes, or until it is golden brown on top and sounds hollow when tapped on the bottom.
10. Cooling and Serving:
    - Remove the bread from the oven and let it cool on a wire rack for at least 30 minutes before slicing.
    - Slice the Artisan Olive Bread and serve it warm or at room temperature. It's delicious on its own or paired with cheese, dips, or a drizzle of olive oil.

This Artisan Olive Bread is full of flavor and has a beautiful rustic crust. Enjoy it as a tasty appetizer, side dish, or snack!

Cheese and Onion Sourdough

Ingredients:

For the Sourdough:

- 1 cup (240g) active sourdough starter
- 1 1/2 cups (360ml) lukewarm water
- 3 1/2 cups (420g) bread flour
- 1 teaspoon salt

For the Cheese and Onion Mix:

- 1 cup (150g) grated cheese (such as cheddar or Gruyère)
- 1/2 cup (75g) finely chopped onion
- 1 tablespoon olive oil

Instructions:

1. Prepare Sourdough:
    - In a large mixing bowl, combine the active sourdough starter and lukewarm water. Stir until the starter is dissolved in the water.
    - Add the bread flour and salt to the bowl. Mix until a shaggy dough forms.
2. Knead Dough:
    - Turn the dough out onto a lightly floured surface. Knead the dough for about 10-15 minutes until it becomes smooth and elastic. Alternatively, you can knead the dough in a stand mixer fitted with a dough hook attachment for 8-10 minutes.
3. First Rise:
    - Place the kneaded dough in a lightly greased bowl. Cover it with a clean kitchen towel or plastic wrap and let it rise in a warm, draft-free place for about 4-6 hours, or until it doubles in size.
4. Prepare Cheese and Onion Mix:
    - While the dough is rising, heat the olive oil in a skillet over medium heat. Add the finely chopped onion and sauté until translucent, about 5-7 minutes. Remove from heat and let it cool.

- Once the sautéed onion has cooled, mix it with the grated cheese in a small bowl. Set aside.

5. Second Rise:
    - Once the dough has doubled in size, gently deflate it by pressing down on it with your fingertips. Transfer it to a lightly floured surface.
    - Spread the cheese and onion mixture evenly over the surface of the dough.
6. Shape Dough:
    - Fold the dough over the cheese and onion mixture and knead it a few times to incorporate the filling. Shape the dough into a round or oval loaf.
7. Final Rise:
    - Place the shaped loaf on a parchment-lined baking sheet or in a proofing basket, seam side down. Cover it loosely with a clean kitchen towel or plastic wrap and let it rise for another 2-3 hours, or until it doubles in size.
8. Preheat Oven:
    - About 20-30 minutes before baking, preheat your oven to 450°F (230°C). Place a baking stone or an overturned baking sheet on the center rack of the oven.
9. Bake:
    - Once the loaf has finished rising, slash the top with a sharp knife or razor blade. Transfer the loaf to the preheated oven and bake for 25-30 minutes, or until it is golden brown on top and sounds hollow when tapped on the bottom.
10. Cooling and Serving:
    - Remove the Cheese and Onion Sourdough Bread from the oven and let it cool on a wire rack for at least 30 minutes before slicing.
    - Slice the bread and serve it warm or at room temperature. It's delicious on its own or paired with soups, salads, or sandwiches.

Enjoy the delightful combination of tangy sourdough, savory cheese, and sweet onions in this Cheese and Onion Sourdough Bread!

Carrot Cake Bread

Ingredients:

- 1 1/2 cups (180g) all-purpose flour
- 1 teaspoon baking powder
- 1/2 teaspoon baking soda
- 1/2 teaspoon salt
- 1 teaspoon ground cinnamon
- 1/2 teaspoon ground nutmeg
- 1/2 cup (120ml) vegetable oil
- 2/3 cup (135g) granulated sugar
- 1/3 cup (70g) packed light brown sugar
- 2 large eggs, room temperature
- 1 teaspoon vanilla extract
- 1 1/2 cups (180g) grated carrots (about 2-3 medium carrots)
- 1/2 cup (60g) chopped walnuts or pecans (optional)
- 1/2 cup (75g) raisins (optional)
- Cream cheese frosting (optional, for topping)

Instructions:

1. Preheat Oven and Prepare Pan:
    - Preheat your oven to 350°F (175°C). Grease a 9x5-inch (23x13cm) loaf pan or line it with parchment paper.
2. Mix Dry Ingredients:
    - In a medium bowl, whisk together the all-purpose flour, baking powder, baking soda, salt, ground cinnamon, and ground nutmeg. Set aside.
3. Mix Wet Ingredients:
    - In a large mixing bowl, whisk together the vegetable oil, granulated sugar, brown sugar, eggs, and vanilla extract until smooth and well combined.
4. Combine Wet and Dry Ingredients:
    - Gradually add the dry ingredients to the wet ingredients, stirring until just combined. Be careful not to overmix.
5. Add Carrots and Optional Ingredients:
    - Fold in the grated carrots until evenly distributed throughout the batter.
    - If using, fold in the chopped nuts and raisins until evenly distributed.

6. Transfer to Pan:
    - Pour the batter into the prepared loaf pan and spread it out evenly.
7. Bake:
    - Bake in the preheated oven for 50-60 minutes, or until a toothpick inserted into the center comes out clean.
8. Cooling:
    - Remove the carrot cake bread from the oven and let it cool in the pan for about 10 minutes. Then transfer it to a wire rack to cool completely.
9. Optional Frosting:
    - Once the bread has cooled completely, you can spread cream cheese frosting over the top if desired.
10. Slice and Serve:
    - Slice the Carrot Cake Bread and serve it as a delicious breakfast, snack, or dessert.

This Carrot Cake Bread is moist, flavorful, and perfect for enjoying the classic taste of carrot cake in a convenient loaf form. Enjoy!

Lemon Poppy Seed Bread

Ingredients:

- 1½ cups (180g) all-purpose flour
- 2 tablespoons poppy seeds
- 1 teaspoon baking powder
- ¼ teaspoon baking soda
- ¼ teaspoon salt
- ½ cup (120ml) vegetable oil or melted butter
- ¾ cup (150g) granulated sugar
- 2 large eggs, room temperature
- ½ cup (120ml) plain yogurt or sour cream
- Zest of 2 lemons
- 2 tablespoons fresh lemon juice
- 1 teaspoon vanilla extract

For the Glaze:

- ½ cup (60g) powdered sugar
- 1-2 tablespoons fresh lemon juice

Instructions:

1. Preheat Oven and Prepare Pan:
   - Preheat your oven to 350°F (175°C). Grease a 9x5-inch (23x13cm) loaf pan or line it with parchment paper.
2. Mix Dry Ingredients:
   - In a medium bowl, whisk together the all-purpose flour, poppy seeds, baking powder, baking soda, and salt. Set aside.
3. Mix Wet Ingredients:
   - In a large mixing bowl, whisk together the vegetable oil or melted butter and granulated sugar until well combined.
   - Add the eggs, one at a time, beating well after each addition.
   - Stir in the plain yogurt or sour cream, lemon zest, lemon juice, and vanilla extract until smooth.

4. Combine Wet and Dry Ingredients:
   - Gradually add the dry ingredients to the wet ingredients, stirring until just combined. Be careful not to overmix.
5. Bake:
   - Pour the batter into the prepared loaf pan and smooth the top with a spatula.
   - Bake in the preheated oven for 45-55 minutes, or until a toothpick inserted into the center comes out clean.
6. Cooling:
   - Remove the lemon poppy seed bread from the oven and let it cool in the pan for about 10 minutes.
   - Then, transfer it to a wire rack to cool completely.
7. Prepare Glaze:
   - In a small bowl, whisk together the powdered sugar and fresh lemon juice until smooth. Adjust the consistency by adding more lemon juice if needed.
8. Drizzle Glaze:
   - Once the bread has cooled, drizzle the glaze over the top.
9. Slice and Serve:
   - Slice the Lemon Poppy Seed Bread and serve it as a delicious breakfast, snack, or dessert.

This Lemon Poppy Seed Bread is moist, flavorful, and perfect for any occasion. Enjoy the bright and citrusy flavors with every bite!

Spelt Bread

Ingredients:

- 3 cups (360g) spelt flour
- 1 packet (7g) active dry yeast
- 1 teaspoon salt
- 1 tablespoon honey or maple syrup
- 1 cup (240ml) warm water
- 2 tablespoons olive oil

Instructions:

1. Activate the Yeast:
    - In a small bowl, combine the warm water and honey or maple syrup. Sprinkle the yeast over the water and let it sit for about 5-10 minutes until frothy.
2. Mix Dough:
    - In a large mixing bowl, combine the spelt flour and salt. Make a well in the center and pour in the activated yeast mixture and olive oil. Stir until a dough forms.
3. Knead the Dough:
    - Turn the dough out onto a lightly floured surface. Knead the dough for about 5-7 minutes until it becomes smooth and elastic. Add more flour if the dough is too sticky.
4. First Rise:
    - Place the kneaded dough in a lightly greased bowl. Cover it with a clean kitchen towel or plastic wrap and let it rise in a warm, draft-free place for about 1 hour, or until it doubles in size.
5. Shape the Loaf:
    - Once the dough has doubled in size, gently punch it down to release the air. Shape the dough into a loaf and place it in a greased or parchment-lined loaf pan.
6. Second Rise:
    - Cover the loaf loosely with a clean kitchen towel or plastic wrap and let it rise for another 30-45 minutes, or until it rises just above the rim of the pan.

7. Preheat Oven:
    - About 20 minutes before baking, preheat your oven to 375°F (190°C).
8. Bake:
    - Once the loaf has finished rising, place it in the preheated oven and bake for 30-35 minutes, or until it is golden brown on top and sounds hollow when tapped on the bottom.
9. Cooling and Serving:
    - Remove the Spelt Bread from the oven and let it cool in the pan for about 10 minutes. Then transfer it to a wire rack to cool completely before slicing.

This Spelt Bread is hearty, nutty, and delicious. Enjoy it fresh with your favorite spreads or use it for sandwiches and toast!

Apple Cinnamon Bread

Ingredients:

- 1 1/2 cups (180g) all-purpose flour
- 1 teaspoon baking powder
- 1/2 teaspoon baking soda
- 1/2 teaspoon salt
- 1 teaspoon ground cinnamon
- 1/4 teaspoon ground nutmeg
- 1/2 cup (115g) unsalted butter, softened
- 2/3 cup (135g) granulated sugar
- 2 large eggs
- 1 teaspoon vanilla extract
- 1/2 cup (120ml) sour cream or Greek yogurt
- 1 1/2 cups (about 2 medium) apples, peeled and diced
- 1/2 cup (60g) chopped walnuts or pecans (optional)

For the Cinnamon Sugar Topping:

- 1/4 cup (50g) granulated sugar
- 1 teaspoon ground cinnamon

Instructions:

1. Preheat Oven and Prepare Pan:
    - Preheat your oven to 350°F (175°C). Grease a 9x5-inch (23x13cm) loaf pan or line it with parchment paper.
2. Mix Dry Ingredients:
    - In a medium bowl, whisk together the all-purpose flour, baking powder, baking soda, salt, ground cinnamon, and ground nutmeg. Set aside.
3. Cream Butter and Sugar:
    - In a large mixing bowl, cream together the softened butter and granulated sugar until light and fluffy.
4. Add Wet Ingredients:
    - Beat in the eggs, one at a time, until well combined. Stir in the vanilla extract.
5. Combine Wet and Dry Ingredients:

- Gradually add the dry ingredients to the wet ingredients, alternating with the sour cream or Greek yogurt. Mix until just combined.
6. Fold in Apples and Nuts:
    - Gently fold in the diced apples and chopped nuts (if using) until evenly distributed throughout the batter.
7. Transfer to Pan:
    - Pour the batter into the prepared loaf pan and spread it out evenly.
8. Prepare Cinnamon Sugar Topping:
    - In a small bowl, mix together the granulated sugar and ground cinnamon for the topping.
9. Top and Bake:
    - Sprinkle the cinnamon sugar mixture evenly over the top of the batter in the loaf pan.
    - Bake in the preheated oven for 50-60 minutes, or until a toothpick inserted into the center comes out clean.
10. Cooling and Serving:
    - Remove the Apple Cinnamon Bread from the oven and let it cool in the pan for about 10 minutes. Then transfer it to a wire rack to cool completely before slicing.

This Apple Cinnamon Bread is moist, fragrant, and perfect for enjoying as a snack or dessert. Serve it warm or at room temperature with a cup of tea or coffee. Enjoy!

Banana Nut Bread

Ingredients:

- 2 cups (240g) all-purpose flour
- 1 teaspoon baking powder
- 1/2 teaspoon baking soda
- 1/2 teaspoon salt
- 1 teaspoon ground cinnamon
- 1/2 cup (115g) unsalted butter, softened
- 3/4 cup (150g) granulated sugar
- 2 large eggs
- 3 ripe bananas, mashed (about 1 1/2 cups)
- 1 teaspoon vanilla extract
- 1/2 cup (60g) chopped walnuts or pecans (optional)

Instructions:

1. Preheat Oven and Prepare Pan:
    - Preheat your oven to 350°F (175°C). Grease a 9x5-inch (23x13cm) loaf pan or line it with parchment paper.
2. Mix Dry Ingredients:
    - In a medium bowl, whisk together the all-purpose flour, baking powder, baking soda, salt, and ground cinnamon. Set aside.
3. Cream Butter and Sugar:
    - In a large mixing bowl, cream together the softened butter and granulated sugar until light and fluffy.
4. Add Wet Ingredients:
    - Beat in the eggs, one at a time, until well combined. Stir in the mashed bananas and vanilla extract.
5. Combine Wet and Dry Ingredients:
    - Gradually add the dry ingredients to the wet ingredients, mixing until just combined. Be careful not to overmix.
6. Fold in Nuts (Optional):
    - Gently fold in the chopped walnuts or pecans, if using, until evenly distributed throughout the batter.
7. Transfer to Pan:

- Pour the batter into the prepared loaf pan and spread it out evenly.
8. Bake:
   - Bake in the preheated oven for 60-70 minutes, or until a toothpick inserted into the center comes out clean. If the top starts to brown too quickly, you can loosely cover it with aluminum foil halfway through baking.
9. Cooling and Serving:
   - Remove the Banana Nut Bread from the oven and let it cool in the pan for about 10 minutes. Then transfer it to a wire rack to cool completely before slicing.

This Banana Nut Bread is moist, flavorful, and perfect for breakfast or as a snack. Enjoy it warm or at room temperature with a spread of butter or cream cheese.

Focaccia with Cherry Tomatoes and Basil

Ingredients:

- 3 1/2 cups (420g) bread flour
- 1 1/2 teaspoons instant yeast
- 1 1/4 cups (300ml) warm water
- 2 tablespoons olive oil, plus extra for drizzling
- 1 teaspoon salt
- 1 pint (about 250g) cherry tomatoes, halved
- Fresh basil leaves, torn
- Coarse sea salt, for sprinkling
- Optional toppings: garlic cloves, olives, grated Parmesan cheese

Instructions:

1. Activate the Yeast:
    - In a small bowl, combine the warm water and instant yeast. Let it sit for about 5-10 minutes until frothy.
2. Mix Dough:
    - In a large mixing bowl, combine the bread flour and salt. Make a well in the center and pour in the activated yeast mixture and olive oil. Stir until a dough forms.
3. Knead the Dough:
    - Turn the dough out onto a lightly floured surface. Knead the dough for about 8-10 minutes until it becomes smooth and elastic. Alternatively, you can knead the dough in a stand mixer fitted with a dough hook attachment for 6-8 minutes.
4. First Rise:
    - Place the kneaded dough in a lightly greased bowl. Cover it with a clean kitchen towel or plastic wrap and let it rise in a warm, draft-free place for about 1-1.5 hours, or until it doubles in size.
5. Prepare Focaccia:
    - Preheat your oven to 425°F (220°C). Grease a 9x13-inch (23x33cm) baking dish or sheet pan with olive oil.

- Once the dough has risen, transfer it to the prepared baking dish. Gently stretch and press the dough to fit the pan. Cover it with a clean kitchen towel and let it rest for about 15-20 minutes.

6. Top the Focaccia:
   - Use your fingertips to create dimples all over the surface of the dough. Drizzle olive oil over the top. Arrange halved cherry tomatoes and torn basil leaves evenly on top of the dough. Press them gently into the dough. Add any optional toppings if desired.
7. Final Rise:
   - Cover the focaccia with a clean kitchen towel and let it rise for another 20-30 minutes, or until slightly puffed.
8. Bake:
   - Sprinkle coarse sea salt over the top of the focaccia.
   - Bake in the preheated oven for 20-25 minutes, or until golden brown and cooked through.
9. Cooling and Serving:
   - Remove the focaccia from the oven and let it cool slightly in the pan before transferring it to a wire rack to cool completely.
   - Slice and serve the Focaccia with Cherry Tomatoes and Basil warm or at room temperature. Enjoy it as a side dish, appetizer, or snack!

This Focaccia with Cherry Tomatoes and Basil is bursting with flavor and makes a delicious addition to any meal. Enjoy the aroma of freshly baked bread filling your kitchen!

www.ingramcontent.com/pod-product-compliance
Lightning Source LLC
LaVergne TN
LVHW061939070526
838199LV00060B/3886